GIRLFRIEND 911

Jacquee Kahn
with
Lori LePage

"I ordered this book on the day it was available. I sat down and read it all in one sitting. It was so eye opening to realize all the things I need to change about the way I behave and the standards I need to set for myself. This is a must have for your survival to dating and a strong relationship! Thanks *Girlfriend 911*, I will keep you posted on the next relationship I enter into and how well I have used my new tools." Laurie S.

"It's amazing how much we women lower our standards for those we love. Jacquee understands how hard it is to breakup and reclaim self-worth. *Girlfriend 911* gives you the tools to move forward. I am really excited that I get to start again and this time use *Girlfriend 911* as my map to a healthy, committed, loving relationship. And yes, it has taken much longer than I would have hoped, but I realize now that I wasn't ready for anything real before." Hayley B.

"I LOVE me some Girlfriend 911. I was introduced to the program when I was going through a broken engagement. It helped me see what I really wanted. By working the program I was able to focus and ask for what I needed. In the end that relationship wasn't for me, but going through the program did bring the honesty and clarity I needed to move on with confidence. Now after a decade I'm back to dating. I keep in mind all the wonderful nuggets in *Girlfriend 911*, and have learned how to set and keep my boundaries. When I feel myself going astray I can easily thumb back through the book and remember all the simple, but truly golden, rules." Jane M.

"This book has been invaluable in terms of recognizing all my past patterns of trying to force square pegs into round holes, and realizing that it really WAS my fault, but in all the best ways possible. I have the power, I just needed (and currently need) to always remember to hang on to it and not squander it away, leaving me only half of me. That will only get me half of what I want. This book also, rightly, eliminates the idea that you can ever be rejected or judged, it just really, clearly shows how all we are is love, and we deserve someone who wants and can give the same love we deserve. A break up is not rejection if you're going about it the Girlfriend 911 way, it just means you're moving forward, closer to what you really deserve, and what will truly make you happy." Erica C.

"After reading Girlfriend 911 and doing the program in this book, my relationship with myself has finally started to change. I really see how I repeat the same patterns in all of my relationships and always end up with the same results. Now in my marriage I am using the Girlfriend 911 approach. I finally feel good about myself and my relationship is changing as a result. There really is nothing like this book. Jacquee Kahn has a true gift. She really understands relationships and how to heal them! Her philosophy is simple; change your behavior, stay connected to your True Self, and everything will fall into place." Paula B.

"It's funny how you have the man and that connection you want, it all seems to fit, but instead of going forward it all goes backwards. You think it's him. For sure it's him. You just have to push a little, or be patient a lot, or stamp your feet and scream, or not do anything that may rock the boat. I tried all four for many years, but after *Girlfriend 911* you realize that each of your actions has an equal and opposite reaction in him. If you want results, then read this book. It will change the way you think and react. I loved how doing the last thing on my list actually worked!!!! It shows you how to be honest and lay down ground rules, and with patience you learn and don't break them. It's surprising what will unfold. For me it's 100 times more than you can ever imagine is possible." Tammy P.

"In no uncertain terms, this book has CHANGED MY LIFE! Before reading *Girlfriend 911* I was on an emotional rollercoaster with my relationship. I was literally in a tumultuous relationship that could have gone on for years! At the point in my life I discovered the *Girlfriend 911* "program," I was at an all-time emotional low. I figured nothing I had done previously had been working, so I was ready to try something different. This book pointed out to me very clearly what I was doing wrong. GF911 helped me get back my power, self confidence, self respect, and establish boundaries with men. It has also helped in so many other types of relationships. It is my daily "mantra" and when I get a little off track, I always refer back to it, because it works!" Belinda J.

TABLE OF CONTENTS

SECTION 1:
WHAT EVERY GIRLFRIEND NEEDS TO KNOW

thinks and tells you, and start looking
within to find the answers.

Are you constantly dating the wrong guys?
Whose fault is it if you allow yourself to be
treated poorly? Instead of feeling bad about
how you've been treated in the past, use those
life lessons to make sure you don't repeat the
mistakes in the future.

Nothing is more important than learning how
to read between the lines rather than believing
everything a man tells you. Pay attention to his
actions, not just his words. When you see red
flags, understand what they are telling you and
act accordingly.

Making the wrong moves can lead to the wrong
kinds of relationships. But making the right
moves can pay off with a strong, healthy long-
term relationship.

SECTION 4:
TOOL KIT

Dedicated to:
Guwi, Me Dud and Bokki

SECTION 1
WHAT EVERY GIRLFRIEND
NEEDS TO KNOW

CHAPTER 1

FROM ONE GIRLFRIEND TO ANOTHER

My friends often refer to me as the "Super Nanny for Women," a nod to Jo Frost, the Mary Poppins–like British parenting expert and TV personality known for her tough-love, no-nonsense approach to raising and disciplining children. I'd casually helped a number of close friends over the years with relationship problems. They told their friends who then told their friends, and so on, and so on. It began to take on a life of its own, and I soon found myself dispensing uncomplicated, straightforward relationship advice to all sorts of women in need.

What makes my perspective different and unique is that I'm not your typical relationship expert; I don't have a degree in psychology or

—

psychiatry. I've never taken a course in human behavior. I'm not a relationship or marriage counselor in the traditional sense. I've never been in therapy, and (ironically) I've never been married nor am I currently in a relationship.

So what makes me qualified to give you advice? Simple. My proven track record. I discovered the formula that has helped countless women find long-lasting, healthy, and happy relationships and rid themselves once and for all of toxic ones. I'm going to share the formula with you in this book, so that no matter what your situation is or how unhealthy your relationship may be, you will have the tools to take control of your love life and create the kind of relationship you've always dreamed of. As with any formula, if you just plug in the right data, you will get the correct result time and time again.

If I still seem an unlikely relationship expert, consider Super Nanny again for a moment. She's an internationally renowned, well-respected child expert, yet she has no children. How can this be? Super Nanny discovered the formula for raising beautifully behaved children. Once she figured it out she applied those same tools with different children in various situations and they worked brilliantly each and every time.

As an English Literature major in college, I was

required to write many papers on famous literary figures. I would get an A+ on almost all of these papers. Not because I was the most creative or most talented writer in the class, but because I discovered the formula to successful writing: by applying the specific structure I was being taught, I was guaranteed a good grade. First, you introduced your thesis stating a point you needed to prove. Second, you used many examples to prove that point. Third, you referred back to your thesis and all the examples you'd used, and tied it all together in a nice neat bow. At the time it never occurred to me it would have any real world application.

Years later, I tried my hand at writing a movie screenplay. I understood the basics. Every story has a beginning, middle, and end. But I was totally clueless and really had no idea that there is a very specific structure and formula for how a great screenplay is written and laid out. I was lucky enough to have a film executive point this out to me after reading my first draft. She recommended a brilliant book that spelled it all out. Once I knew the formula and *applied* it, I could look at any screenplay and immediately fix it. The formula was one thing—but the *secret* was to *apply* it. For a time I turned it into a career of sorts; I would read other people's screenplays and using the tried and true formula, help them to make a structurally dysfunctional script, great.

It wasn't long before I applied those same principles to relationships and I discovered what would become the Girlfriend 911 formula. Based on my past experiences with formulas, I knew it would work in any and every situation. It didn't matter how different or varied the circumstances were, the outcome was always the same. And as the expert, I didn't have to be married. I didn't even have to be in a relationship. As long as I had the formula, I could give it to anyone seeking relationship advice because I knew beyond a shadow of a doubt it would work, with one caveat—*they would have to apply it.*

MY STORY

I wasn't always the go-to relationship guru. Over the years I'd made the same dating and relationship mistakes every other woman had made; settling for less than I deserved, and generally giving the guys I dated a free pass on bad behavior. So how did I make the necessary changes and turn my life around? Three very important lessons:

Life Lesson #1: Listen to your mother. I didn't. I like to think I just forgot some of what she had told my sister and me early on: See things as they are, not as you wish them to be. Stay true to yourself. Work on yourself first, all other relationships will flow from that. She didn't want us to be desperate women looking for a man to define or save us. But I never forgot what she told us about soul mates. She said that in a union of true soul mates, the whole is greater than the sum of its parts. Each person benefits and flourishes in a way they could never do on their own. In such a relationship neither partner should ever have to compromise being who they are; rather, each should support the other. True soul mates magnify and amplify each other's life experiences simply by being together. As a result, I had no interest in being in a relationship unless it was absolutely the right person, the right timing, and the right situation. I didn't need to be rescued or taken care of. I knew there was someone out there who would enhance my enjoyment of life and I would do the same for him. It was simple. So I happily got on with my life—until Mr. F arrived. (But more about him in a minute....)

Life Lesson #2 came from, of all places, a movie. When I was in my mid-twenties, I saw the movie *Emma,* based on the novel by Jane Austen. As an English Literature major I thought I was pretty well-versed in all things Austen. But when I saw *Emma* all those years later, I was particularly struck—as if for the first time—by the notion of real romance and that delicate courtship dance between men and women so perfectly captured in Austen's stories. I came out of that movie completely taken with the idea of getting back to that bygone romantic era: men were to court women, women were to allow themselves to be wooed and pursued, and dignity and respect were once again to be the cornerstones upon which healthy relationships were built. It was, as they say, a "lightbulb moment," all I had to do was update it for the 21st Century! Unfortunately, there was one more lesson I needed to learn—a big one—before I could put my mother's wisdom and Emma's guidance into practice.

This particular lesson, Life Lesson #3, my story of Mr. F is essentially the original case study for my Girlfriend 911 program. Mr. F was my nickname for him and is the name I will use for the purposes of this book. We met through a mutual friend. He actually called me for professional advice as we were both working in the movie industry at the time. He was looking for a job and I often heard of available positions. What should have been a ten-minute phone conversation turned into a three-hour-long marathon. Instinctively, I knew something was special here. Unfortunately for me, he had just come out of a seven-year relationship and wanted to be free. I, on the other hand, was in my late twenties and ready to start thinking about settling down. The chemistry was undeniable. He just "got me" like no one else ever had, and that was intoxicating and hard to let go of, even though we clearly were not on the same page. He couldn't, or wouldn't, fully commit, and so I accepted a "friends with benefits" situation, hoping against hope that he would see the light and finally step up. He was like a drug I just couldn't quit.

After a tumultuous five-year, on-again-off-again "situation" between us, he met a woman whom he would later marry. I was completely and absolutely devastated. When he told me he had started dating someone and thought it could be serious, I was finally jerked back into reality and all those lessons learned from my mother came into play. Of course, I should have been using them from the first day I met him, but I was so "in love" that I let my high standards slip and couldn't see the forest for the trees. He was very reluctant to let me go. He still wanted to be "friends," but we both knew what that meant.

At this point, I finally realized it was time to get him out of my life for good. I had tried many times in the past, but had been weak and had always gone back on my threats. I knew that unless I did something drastic, history would repeat itself. We had an amazing connection, incredible chemistry, and we enjoyed each other's company a lot. So even if I tried to get him out of my life, I knew it wouldn't be long before he'd be reaching out, wanting to do the "friends" thing while still dating this new girl. For five years, that exact reality had played out. For my own sanity, I just couldn't allow this to go on any longer.

This particular life lesson was the genesis for my formula, and it's what really started the whole Girlfriend 911 program. I began to recognize for the first time the nature of men and what made them tick. I discovered quite accidentally that his behavior was, in fact, wholly dependent upon mine. So here's what I did. This is really important, so pay attention!

In hopes of scaring the living daylights out of him, and ensuring that I never heard from him again, I came up with a foolproof plan. As they say, desperate times call for desperate measures. I sent him an email that expressed for the very first time, in a clear and concise manner, exactly how I felt about him. I told him that I wanted to marry him and if he didn't feel the same way, he absolutely couldn't be in my life in any form or fashion. I was certain that this kind of honesty was a sure-fire guarantee that he wouldn't be contacting me ever again—the nail in the coffin, so to speak. I was utterly exhausted and emotionally bankrupt. I had to get my life and my self-respect back before he completely destroyed me.

My plan worked perfectly. I had laid all my cards on the table. He told me he was sad and wished we could still "just be friends." I am sure if I'd chosen that option, "just friends" would've have ended up as "just lovers." No matter how badly I had behaved in the past where Mr. F was concerned, being his mistress and being second best was never going to be an option. Although he cared about me deeply and understood where I was coming from, he wasn't on the same page. We both walked away and out of each other's lives.

For me, it was incredibly painful and devastating. Putting the sexual stuff aside, he was one of my closest friends. Losing him was like losing a piece of my heart. I grieved appropriately and then tried to get on with my life. It was a long and difficult process, but what I started to notice was that for the first time in a long time, I was back in the driver's seat. I felt totally empowered and in control. It was like this huge burden had been lifted off my shoulders. Emotionally, I had been completely stripped down and had gotten to my absolute truth. It wasn't just out there in some nebulous etheric realm; I had written it down, given it form. He couldn't say he'd misunderstood me; there it was in black and white in that email. The fact that he didn't reciprocate the feelings almost didn't matter. I felt really good about myself for the first time in a long time.

Baring my soul in that way was completely liberating, and it gave me the strength and determination to stick to my plan to sever all ties to him, when...after a few months, to my complete surprise, he reached out!

My honesty and my actions had apparently had the complete opposite effect on him! Go figure! He said he missed me and wanted me back in his life as "friends." But this time it was different. I was different.

I held firm to my new standards and boundaries and said, "Absolutely not. It's all or nothing. You either commit to being in my life one hundred percent or you can't be in it at all." This was not meant as an ultimatum at all; it was a simple statement of *truth* about the choice I was making, and it left him to decide what he wanted to do about it. My absence had left him in such a tailspin that he suddenly couldn't get enough of me and continuously reached out in the hopes I would change my mind. But I didn't. Never in a million years would I ever have anticipated this kind of reaction from him. He did the exact opposite of what I expected him to do. I thought I'd discovered the Holy Grail!

Although he did disappear for a while—a few months, as I said—after he'd had time to process the situation, he realized he missed me terribly. The more I held firm to my boundaries, the more it challenged him, and the more he wanted me. For reasons I am not going to go into, he could not marry me, (he's explained it to me, and although I don't agree, I respect his choice) but his feelings for me haven't changed to this day. In fact, they've gotten stronger. I know this because he's continued to get in touch with me over the years and let me know in no uncertain terms how he feels about me and the kind of impact I've had on his life. He never once told me any of this when we were actually together.

I realized that when I wasn't true to myself, he wasn't true to me. Truth is the key. When I bared my soul, he bared his as well, even though it took time. What an important lesson. Thank you, Mr. F, for all that you've taught me.

FROM ME TO YOU

Since getting Mr. F out of my life, many other women have followed in my footsteps. They have experienced similar results by taking their power back just as I did. That's the whole idea behind the Girlfriend 911 program. Soon, one girlfriend told another about my program and before I knew it, I was counseling clients (for lack of a better term) and seeing amazing results.

My goal all along has been very simple: help single women find a healthy, loving, committed, monogamous, and honest relationship, and help women currently in relationships maintain healthy ones or free themselves from toxic ones. My approach has been equally simple: teach women that healthy and mutually satisfying relationships are built on respect, firm standards and boundaries, and belief in one's True Self. These basics make up the core of my Girlfriend 911 program.

Those of you who adhere to my program will inevitably succeed and walk away with your self-respect, confidence, and dignity intact. For those of you who are lacking these important qualities, I'll show you how to get them. You will always be *in your power*, you will know how to set appropriate standards and boundaries, and you will never allow yourself to be taken for granted again.

Women tend to make crucial mistakes in the dating arena, simply because they haven't been taught what to do. Time and time again, we wind up settling for something I like to refer to as "crumbs." We will delve into this a little later, but know that being in your truth and not settling for crumbs are two very important factors throughout this process. No more crumbs, ladies! You deserve the whole crumpet.

In order to do that, you're going to be required to change your old habits and thought patterns immediately. You *must* follow the rules carefully and *surrender* to the process! There will be no compromise! There is only *one way*. We live in a world of instant gratification, but relationships are not instant. We're talking about your life partner here. You need to stay focused on the big picture. If you're looking for a long-term relationship, you can't think in terms of immediate results.

Just like in the movies, you will eventually get the guy. Not just any guy, but a man you are truly connected to, and a man who is worthy of you. This may or may not be the man you are with now. The answer to that will reveal itself during the course of the program. If you are currently dating someone, you will either end up in a healthy relationship with this person, or you will get him out of your life completely—for good—if he's not right for you. By following the steps of my program, you will know where you stand, and how your man truly feels about you. It is not an easy process, but it's a rewarding one, once you get to the other side. If you're not dating anyone at the moment, then your timing is impeccable. You will save yourself from making, and/or repeating, many common and potentially catastrophic mistakes, so long as you stick to my rules and do not "go rogue" on me.

By the end of my program, you will understand your worth and know beyond a shadow of a doubt what you deserve in life, and what you deserve in a relationship. And by doing so, you are opening the path to greater things in all areas of your life. If you choose not to follow my program, you must be satisfied knowing that you will just continue to get more of what you've always gotten, or perhaps even worse.

Obviously, what you've been doing up until this point isn't working, or you wouldn't be considering my program. Have the courage to face the truth in your relationship, and do something about it. It's been said that Albert Einstein defined insanity as doing the same thing over and over again and expecting different results. Unless you change your behavior, you will never be able to change the result—that's a guarantee! Since you're already reading this book, you've probably figured out that part. Now, all you need are the tools to bring about these incredible changes, so read on.

In case you're wondering how I came up with

the Girlfriend 911 title—I didn't! One of my girlfriends named me that after she had literally called me for emergency love help at all hours of the day and night.

Since then, however, I've come to recognize how truly apt the name was because the greatest friend any of us can have is that little voice inside us, our gut instinct, our True Self, our very own individual Girlfriend 911. She's on duty 24/7 to help and guide us, and so long as we listen, she will *never* let us down.

By reading *Girlfriend 911*, you've taken the first major step in changing your life for the better. You should be very proud of yourself and feel energized and excited. Soon you will have a whole new way of being in the world that is going to bring the most incredible and surprisingly positive changes in other aspects of your life as well. Having standards and boundaries and knowing you deserve only the best from those around you can be applied in all areas of your life; work situations, relationships with friends and family, and how you raise your children.

To help you stay on track, keep referring back to the book, as I will be there guiding you step-by-step. It's always hard to change your behavior when you've been doing it one way (the wrong way) for so long, but it's definitely not impossible.

—

Practice will make perfect.

My friends and clients have been kind enough to give me permission to share their stories with you. All names contained in this book have been changed. I hope when reading these stories you realize you're not alone. Chances are, someone else has made the same mistakes you have. By sharing their stories we hope we can help other women, and that *together* we can change what's going on with women, dating, and relationships—**one girlfriend at a time!**

CHAPTER 2

HOW DID YOU GET HERE, GIRLFRIEND?

If you're in a satisfying, fulfilling relationship where both of you are on the same page, you want the same things from the relationship, and it's heading in a direction you both want, then you don't need this program. If, however, you are in a relationship that is not working and needs fixing, or you are seeking a healthy, committed relationship, then this is absolutely the program for you. My program will provide the tools you need to reclaim yourself, clearly define who you are and what you want in a man, and establish strict standards and firm boundaries for how you will conduct yourself in a relationship. But you have to put in the time and effort to get the results you want. Otherwise it won't work.

The most important first step is to take a look at how you got here. You can't move forward until you spend some time looking back at your dating habits and relationship patterns. So, how did you get here? It's my opinion that the dating world is such a mess because nobody knows what role they are supposed to be playing anymore. You may not want to hear it, but none of this is the fault of the men. They are only following suit. Men are getting away with bad behavior *only* because we women have allowed them to. We are responsible for *ourselves*. If we are being treated poorly by a man then it's because we are saying (explicitly or implicitly) it's alright with us, even when it's not. All boundaries have been completely dropped. We are rewarding bad behavior. Women are becoming increasingly desperate for companionship, and rather than putting our collective foot down when we aren't treated respectfully, we are letting men get away with it. Of course, this gives men all of the power. Most of the time men don't realize they are doing anything wrong, and how could they? We don't let our children or our friends get away with treating us so poorly, so why would we let grown men get away with it?

As I started to observe the dynamics between men and women, I immediately noticed that so many women have absolutely no self-worth when it comes to dealing with men and don't believe they deserve very much in relationships. This is not an insult, but an honest observation. These beautiful, strong, talented women could be superstars in the workforce and confidants to their friends. They could juggle careers and life and could succeed at anything they set their minds to, and yet when it came to men and relationships, they would systematically fail. Even high-powered women, savvy enough to close multi-million-dollar deals, can't always close the deal in a relationship. They have no problem being equal adversaries with men in the boardroom and yet in the bedroom they cede their power all too quickly for fear of losing him.

From my experience, I have found that women today are trying so hard to be modern women and "have it all" that they've lost themselves. They have no idea what they want, what they need, and, most importantly, what they *deserve*, when it comes to relationships. Today's women present themselves on a silver platter for the taking, whatever the men want, whenever they want it, and however they want it. Where is the challenge and the turn-on in that?

The Equal Rights Movement, it seems to me, is to blame for this imbalance. Before you throw your arms up in the air, hear me out. I'm all for equality, but women are fighting so hard to be on a level playing field with men, both professionally and personally, that their romantic lives suffer. Women are now dating men like they *are* men. Women are asking guys out on dates, making the first move, being overly aggressive, and in many cases, being overly promiscuous, too. The lines have become blurred and men have become extremely confused. Clearly, this has to change in order for relationships to succeed. I've heard one nightmare story after another; dating is miserable, men are fickle and refuse to commit, everyone is cheating on everyone, marriages are crumbling, and women are settling for fear of being alone. It's a mess! All of this is unacceptable to me and should be unacceptable to you as well.

Why don't women today understand what they are worth? They settle for far less than they deserve, they accept or overlook bad behavior, and they transform themselves into the women they think their partners want them to be. And when one relationship fails, they move on to the next one, where chances are they end up repeating the same mistakes over and over again. I've discovered there are a number of reasons women do this:

1: SELF-WORTH

Women today have forgotten what they're worth. They neglect or diminish what they have to offer in favor of what they think men want. They ignore their own wants and needs and replace them with their partner's wants and needs. The dictionary defines self-worth as "the sense of one's own value or worth as a person." Not to be confused with self-confidence, self-worth is our innate ability to recognize in ourselves all that we have to offer, and therefore, all that we deserve. Identifying and acknowledging your own self-worth is not always easy, especially for women. Sometimes even the smartest, prettiest, most successful and accomplished women struggle to find and acknowledge their own self-worth. However, it's a critical step on the road to a healthy relationship. Once you clearly define and claim your own self-worth, you gain the self-respect and inner confidence to set your sights on what you deserve. People who truly respect themselves rarely make bad relationship choices.

Take, for example, my friend Lisa. She was 29 when she got married, and although she was beautiful inside and out, and had so much to offer, unfortunately she didn't see it that way. She had no self-worth and married the first guy that came along. He was way beneath her. Her friends were shocked that she would even date a guy like that, as no one could see what she saw in him. Lisa met him in her early twenties, and several years later when he proposed, she said yes. This despite her confession to me that not only was she not in love with this man, but she'd never really had any true feelings for him. Ouch!

Unfortunately, we all know a Lisa. We see Lisas every day. In fact you might be a Lisa reading this. The problem with Lisa was that she didn't believe in herself. She didn't think she could do any better. She didn't believe she was worthy or deserving of an absolutely great guy. She told me she was marrying him because *he* loved *her*, and this may be the only man that ever would. She compromised her own happiness for all the wrong reasons, and of course she was completely miserable and the marriage fell apart. They got divorced and Lisa was fortunate to be given a second chance to find her true love the right way. She adhered to the Girlfriend 911 program and she's doing better than ever! You'd be amazed at how strong and empowered Lisa is today.

2: FEAR

Fear drives many women to make poor decisions. Fear of being alone; fear that we won't find someone to love us; fear we'll be judged by our girlfriends, our families, society; fear of stating our truth; fear of setting boundaries; fear of commanding respect; and fear of standing up for ourselves. The fear of not getting married is a powerful motivator. It often leads women to choose *Mr. Right Now* over *Mr. Right*. This is what I like to call "stability, no passion"—when women choose stability over chemistry and connection, love that is planned and thought out, and therefore not "love" at all. These women "think" love and don't "feel" it.

I'm here to tell you that you can't love with your head. You can only love with your heart. These women are in such a hurry to get married that they settle for the first stable guy who comes along, instead of waiting for the person that is right for *them* to show up.

A few years ago, *Cosmopolitan* magazine took a survey that found that most women would rather *knowingly* marry the wrong guy and get divorced, than not get married at all. Sad to think that despite all the advances women have made over the years, there is still such a stigma attached to being a single woman.

Unfortunately, I know a lot of girlfriends, too many, who've gone from one bad relationship to another. Instead of taking time out from dating and figuring out what part they're playing in the failure of these relationships, they just move on to the next one hoping for a better result. Fear totally and completely drives them. They have tunnel vision. They want to get married, they want to have children, and so all the things that should be important in finding Mr. Right and having a healthy and happy relationship go on the back burner. What becomes front and center is just "closing the deal." Of course, once they're actually married, reality sets in and more times than not, they end up divorced.

I lost my good friend, Kelli, in just this type of scenario. I was in my late twenties. This was pre–Girlfriend 911 and long before I knew anything about relationships, but my common sense told me this was not going to end well. Kelli was one of my closest friends at the time. She had everything going for her. She was a super smart attorney, had a great personality, and was gorgeous to boot. The only thing missing was Mr. Right.

Kelli's last relationship was toxic and emotionally abusive and she vowed to never let that happen to her again. From the first day she met Matthew, I knew it was a disaster waiting to happen, but Kelli was getting impatient. She'd been online dating for about a year and hadn't met anyone. Her thirties were rapidly approaching, she wanted to have kids, and as she told me many times, she didn't want to be single and alone. She was operating out of total and complete fear. She chose to ignore many red flags (I talk about red flags extensively in Chapter 6). Matthew was amazing on paper; he came from a good family, was well-educated, made a decent living—all things that were important to Kelli. The reality, however, was a different story. He was an ass, plain and simple. He abused Kelli emotionally and treated her horribly. Eventually, as her best friend, I couldn't sit back and watch this go on any longer. I desperately tried to reason with her and make her see the truth, but to no avail. She was set on marrying this man. No matter what I said or did, or the examples I provided for how he was mistreating her, she couldn't and wouldn't hear it. I was left with no choice but to end the friendship.

I realized it was very hard for me to respect Kelli when she clearly had no respect for herself. I heard through mutual friends she married Matthew a few years later. I was surprised because when we were still friends she told me that every time she'd brought up the subject of marriage, Matthew didn't want to talk about it. I also heard that three years after they got married, they got divorced. Amongst many other things, he'd been cheating on her. By this time, Kelli had had two children and was forced to go back to work because Matthew didn't want to pay for anything and was suing her for alimony. My heart broke for her, as I absolutely knew if only she hadn't operated out of fear, this whole mess could have so easily been avoided.

3: FAIRYTALES

I'm not sure how the notion of a "fairytale romance" still exists in this day and age, but I constantly hear women talking about their "Prince Charming" or their "happily ever after." Women often say they want their men to treat them like a "princess."

Fairytales are pure fantasy, and as such, they couldn't possibly compete with reality. There's no such thing as perfect. "Perfection" is an unrealistic, unattainable goal. Seeking perfection will inevitably lead to disappointment. If that is your expectation, you've failed before you've even begun. Sorry to burst your bubble, but let's get back to reality here.

We are brought up to believe that marriage is supposed to be picture-perfect, but that is another misconception. Only a picture can be perfect, because it is still, and captures a perfect moment in time. If you believed in Santa Claus, at some point in your life you were horribly disappointed. If you believe in Prince Charming and fairytale relationships, the same holds true.

The most famous modern day "fairytale" was the marriage of Prince Charles to Princess Diana. Boy did we all fall for that one hook, line, and sinker! Not only was Diana a real princess, but she had all the things that fairytales are made of; she was regal and beautiful, she lived in a real-life castle, she had tons of money and her own Prince Charming. Unfortunately, as we later came to discover when it all unraveled, not one of these things made her happy. The reality of Princess Diana's situation was actually quite shocking, and was about as far from our notion of a fairytale as one could get.

When it comes to marriage and relationships, you need to be realistic. Don't wish for something unattainable and untrue, like a fairytale. Instead, create something *real*, where all of your needs and wants are met in *your* reality, not someone else's fantasy. The best we can hope for is a strong and healthy relationship, not a perfect one. A strong and healthy relationship is one where you have high standards and firm boundaries. There is mutual respect for one another, and you both learn to communicate with each other and work through your problems. You will learn all of this, and more, when you follow my Girlfriend 911 program!

I can't end this chapter without discussing two other factors that contributed to how we got here. They might be less important, but I think they are equally culpable. They have seeped into our collective female consciousness and caused the erosion of true romance and healthy, happy relationships.

4: MODERN TECHNOLOGY

Technology, as wonderful as it is, has caused a major reduction in our communication skills, and, unfortunately, has been a great contributor to the death of romance. Sure, it's much easier to text and email, but it really takes the personal factor out of relationships.

To quote a friend of mine, texting is like "lyrics without the music." You only get part of the communication, as the emotional component is lacking, and so much gets lost in translation. Texting should *not* replace phone conversations or face-to-face dating. Anyone can appear to be witty and smart over text and email. A real conversation is the best way to really get to know someone and to build chemistry and intimacy. Texting has become an excuse to reach out to someone without having to invest any time or effort in a real conversation. Especially in the beginning of a relationship, when you're just starting to get to know someone, texting should be used minimally and should never replace genuine interaction.

I have a couple of clients who had guys in their lives that were just texting them and never asking them out. I mean, for *weeks* they were texting back and forth and there was *never* an invitation to actually be taken out on a date! Ladies, this is totally unacceptable. If you meet a man and he starts out by texting you, he better ask you out within a couple of days, or the texting needs to "*cease*" (activity has to stop) and "*desist*" (activity can't be taken up again later). No point wasting your precious time and valuable energy on a man who has no intention of ever moving forward beyond a text message.

If he's not asking you out within a reasonable amount of time, one week tops, feel free to either ignore his texts, or spell it out for him. For example, you can let him know that you're not going to be responding to his texts anymore, as he doesn't seem to have any interest in asking you out, and you're looking for a long-term relationship. That should give him great clarity. Either you'll never hear from him again, or he'll step up and ask you out. Ignoring the text altogether can bring out his true colors as well. He will notice something is wrong and may very well step up on his own. If he's the kind of man who gets *angry* when you don't respond, run for the hills! Consider yourself lucky to have found this out now.

5: MODERN MEDIA

Reality shows such as *The Bachelor, Jersey Shore,* and *Temptation Island,* to name a few, are wildly entertaining. I enjoy these guilty pleasures as much as the next person, but they're exploitative and never portray women or relationships in a favorable, realistic light. In fact, quite the opposite. Most of the women on these shows dress provocatively, have no standards or boundaries, and degrade themselves to get the attention of one or more guys. It's embarrassing and cringe-worthy to watch, and not the kind of message we should be sending to all the millions of women watching these shows.

The same can be said of reality stars who become famous because of sex tapes that were "accidentally" leaked. Again, this kind of behavior shouldn't be rewarded and celebrated in our culture; I think that's pretty obvious. It's no wonder many young girls think it's okay to dress like prostitutes, have no respect for themselves, sleep with a bunch of different guys, and then post it on the Internet for all to see. How are you ever going to be able to find a long-term, healthy, committed and honest relationship when this is what's out there, and considered the norm?

If you recognize yourself in any of the above, you should by now have a clearer picture of how you got here. The good news is, you don't have to stay here! Girlfriend 911 will give you self-worth, stop you from operating out of fear, deliver you from Fairytale Land into reality, force you to engage in real-life conversations and not rely on modern technology, and make sure you present yourself in a respectful ladylike manner. All these bad habits and behavior patterns are changeable. You don't have to be *here* any longer!!!

Before you can move forward, however, you'll need to take some important steps to prepare yourself:

Recognize your mistakes, missteps, and old patterns.

- Take responsibility.

- Make the decision to put a stop to whatever

habits and/or behaviors aren't working.

- Clarify what it is you want moving forward and commit to doing the work to make it happen.

You are now ready to reclaim your power in relationships, the Girlfriend 911 way!

CHAPTER 3

MEN ARE HUNTERS, GIRLFRIENDS ARE GATHERERS

In order for dating and relationships to work, you have to allow men to take on the role of men and women to take on the role of *women*. Men are born to be hunters, chasers, and pursuers—plain and simple. Men are hard-wired to be powerful, independent, and aggressive; behaviors that can be traced back to prehistoric times when men were actual hunters and protectors and women were gatherers and assemblers. Men need to be allowed to pound their chests and feel like men. Women, on the other hand, are meant to be hunted, chased, and pursued. It's our job to gather the facts and assemble a healthy relationship.

Men and women are wired differently. We all know this. I'm not saying that a woman's place is in the kitchen, by any stretch of the imagination, but I am saying that ladies need to act like ladies. Men need to court women, and women need to allow the men to court them.

We don't have to be completely old-fashioned. It is the twenty-first century, after all, but it's important to fully understand that women are designed to be nurturers and caretakers. We are made to bear children and care for our families. Men today have become completely emasculated by our inability to allow them to be providers. Of course we can still work hard and have our own careers, but we cannot take everything away from men when it comes to dating and marriage.

Certainly, a handful of lazy men out there would much rather have a woman do everything, and they are never going to change. If you happen to have one of those perched on your couch right now, read on, girlfriend. Read on!

I personally believe there is nothing more romantic than being courted by a man, especially in that beginning phase when you're getting to know each other. It can be totally exhilarating. If you've never tried it this way, it's time you do.

Let the man ask you out on a proper date, get dressed up, have him pick you up (assuming it's safe and you haven't just met on the Internet), have him choose the restaurant, let him pay (yes, at least the first few dates), and watch the evening unfold. If you enjoy your time, you do it again. This is how we explore each other and test our chemistry. Doing this makes the man feel like a real man, and you are being treated like a lady. This is a very good start.

Attraction and romance have to build. The more time you give it to build up, the more explosive it will be when you take it to the next level.

If a man doesn't date properly, he's not the man for you. I think this is worth repeating: If a man doesn't date properly, *he's* not the man for you! We women are so creative at convincing ourselves that he *could* be the man for us that we tend to let bad behavior slide. We find all sorts of excuses to continue dating these men, because we have no standards and no boundaries. We come across as desperate, and frankly, quite pathetic. It's a harsh assessment, I know, but one that I've observed time and time again. When, ladies, did we become so disempowered and pitiful?

It's time your man learns how to court his woman properly; otherwise, he needs to find someone else to "hang out" with. Sorry, but if you don't have standards or boundaries, how can you expect a man to know where you stand? As the famous saying goes, "If you don't stand for something, you'll fall for anything." We will get heavily into standards and boundaries later on, but for now, just remember that you must expect and allow a true courtship to take place before any relationship ensues.

Do not ever court a man! The romance ends entirely the second a woman takes the lead. I'm not asking women to be helpless or naive; quite the contrary. We definitely need to be strong and confident. This is all about balance, remember, but we do not need to do the man's job for him. Women may think that they are empowered to believe they don't need to wait for a guy to call, or that they are a man's equal and should take the bull by the horns, but when women become over-bearing, they actually become completely dis-empowered, and typically, quite unattractive to a man.

CHAPTER 4

A GIRLFRIEND'S GUIDE TO SELF

If you're reading my book, you recognize that what you've been doing isn't working and you're serious about wanting to make changes in your life. Consider this your wake-up call. It's time for a reality check; let go of old behaviors, patterns, and habits, and figure out who you really want to be with. Stop making excuses. Put aside what everyone else thinks and tells you and start looking within—to your True Self—to find the answers.

When I am connected to my truth—operating from a completely truthful, authentic place—I call that my True Self. Your True Self is your gut, your instinct, your soul. It's your purest, most honest, most genuine part of who you are. Your True Self is the *true you*. The True Self exists in everyone.

Unfortunately, we are influenced by other

people's ideas and opinions, and as time goes on it becomes more and more difficult to tap into our own True Selves. Society starts telling us what we should think, what we should wear, what we should do, who we should become. The media tells us what's beautiful and what is not. Our friends tell us how we need to act. We often get in relationships and change in order to please our partners. In no time at all, we lose our True Selves. Rather than operating from our True Selves—who we really are—we operate from what I call our False Selves—the self that everyone else thinks we *should* be. The first step on my program is to reconnect with your True Self and start the journey from a completely authentic place. It's impossible to attract and maintain a healthy relationship if you're not connected with your True Self.

Whenever you're making a comparison of "better than" or "worse than," you're operating out of your False Self. Your True Self just is. It doesn't compare itself to anything else. If you've ever met someone connected to their True Self, you will notice that they're not affected by their environment or the people who surround them. They are at peace with who they are, and they don't sweat the small stuff. It doesn't matter if they are wealthy or poor, beautiful or plain. They are just happy being themselves. The Girlfriend 911

—

40

program forces you to connect with your True Self. When you are in your truth, you feel strong, in control, and empowered.

Put your boxing gloves on, ladies. It's False Self vs. True Self! By taking the steps to tell your man exactly how you feel and what you want from your relationship, you will cut through the BS, get out of denial, and get down to your basic truth, your True Self. This gives him the gift of choice and gives you the courage to let him go if he really doesn't feel the same way. It also allows for him to come back into your life when the timing is right, and you and he are both ready.

It's my opinion that most people on the planet today operate out of their False Selves, and as a result, nothing is what it appears to be. We are constantly fed lies, and it's hard to figure out fact from fiction. People just don't tell the truth anymore, and it's become almost an acceptable practice to lie and cheat, especially when it comes to relationships. No one has any idea what the real truth is or where they stand. No one is willing to dig deep to find their truth and state it. Everybody is operating out of their False Selves. Our celebrity culture seems to be the biggest culprit of lies versus truth.

We are constantly being fed these so-called picture-perfect couples in their picture-perfect relationships only to watch it all come crashing down. We buy into the fantasy. I think if these celebrities were operating more out of their True Selves and less out of their False Selves, this would not be happening nearly as much. When you are in your truth and connected to your True Self you can only make great choices, and the best part is that you will recognize Mr. Wrong almost immediately.

OPPOSITE DAY

Most men operate from their heads. When you do things the Girlfriend 911 way, you force them to operate from their hearts (from a place of truth). When a man is in his truth, he says what he means and means what he says. What he says matches what he does; his words and his actions are congruent.

Unfortunately, a lot of men say one thing and do another. I like to call this behavior "Opposite Day." I got the idea from my friend's little boy who explained to me that if you say no when you really mean yes, or you say you're sad when you're really happy, it's Opposite Day. I thought this was so hysterical that I began to use his term to define how men think and act, especially when it comes to women and relationships. Men very often think or talk themselves right out of a relationship because they rely on "logic" or "practical" reasoning, instead of relying on their knowingness and their truth.

Men get really confused when it's *real*. Very often they just aren't emotionally mature enough or ready to settle down. They get scared and want to protect themselves from facing their truth, so instead of operating out of their hearts, they operate out of their heads. Even though you are convinced he truly loves you, he tells you he doesn't, just to protect himself. That's Opposite Day. Most of my clients have had their man admit they were in love with them, or admit that this was "the real deal," and then turn and run away a minute later. This is what they do. Doesn't it make you feel better already knowing that it's Opposite Day? Now everything should start to make more sense.

When you're experiencing Opposite Day, it's important to pay attention to his actions as well as his words. If he says one thing and does another, it's Opposite Day. For example, if he tells you he doesn't want to be in a committed relationship and just wants to be friends, yet he's calling you all the time and can't seem to live without you, his actions don't match his words. In this scenario, his actions are his truth—his True Self—showing you his real feelings. His words are his lies—his False Self—trying to convince you (and more importantly, himself), why it won't work out. The flip side of this is when a man tells you he loves you, says all the right things, and then runs for the hills. This is an example of a guy who's most likely really scared and unable to live the truth that he speaks. Either way his actions and his words don't match.

My Girlfriend 911 program will show you how to always operate from your True Self. When you're operating out of a place of truth, you either force your man to come up to your level and be in his truth as well, or you don't allow him into your life. It's that simple. If a man is really not into you, and is telling you and showing you that he's not, he's probably telling you the truth. If you are in your truth, you will recognize the difference and be able to let go and move on.

When you're connected to your True Self is when I believe you can truly attract your soul mate. Throughout the book I may refer to the perfect partner for you as your soul mate, for lack of a better term. Your soul mate is the one person in this world who is right for you, with whom you connect on all levels; emotionally, physically, mentally, and spiritually. If one or more of these connections is missing, this is *not* your soul mate, and you should keep looking until he comes along.

CHAPTER 5

IT'S YOUR FAULT, GIRLFRIEND, SO OWN IT!

The reason you are in this situation is not because you are with a guy who refuses to commit to you, or a guy who treats you badly. The reason you are in this situation has everything to do with *you*. In other words, it's *all your fault*.

Most women get angry when I tell them this, as no one likes to be blamed for anything. I understand this is a hard concept to understand, but here's the truth: everything that you've put on the guy up to this point as his fault, you need to put back on yourself as your fault, and *own it*. Point the finger back at yourself. Stop living in what I call the bubble defense: "It's not me, it's everyone else. I just keep picking the wrong guys."

If you've been in a bunch of relationships that haven't worked out, guess what, it's not about the guy; it's about *you*. Your behavior has not been up to par, and you have allowed him to get away with anything and everything.

Instead of looking at past relationships as negatives, look at them as positives, and learn from your mistakes. So, ladies, change your behavior, and your men will change theirs! It's that simple. If you can do that, you're ready for my program.

STANDARDS

Over the years, I've spoken to a lot of women: my own girlfriends, their girlfriends, and so on. It became very clear to me that women had no standards and were providing men with whatever they wanted, whenever they wanted it.

This has to stop, and should be the first step in changing your behavior. You must set some standards for yourself. When exactly the shift came from women holding something sacred and special and men chasing after it, to women giving it away for free, I don't know, but I suspect the Sexual Revolution, Equal Rights, and the invention of the birth control pill all had something to do with it.

Standards describe what you will and won't tolerate in a relationship. Once you create a high set of standards for yourself, you must vow to absolutely never break them. Breaking them means lowering your standards, which will compromise your level of respect, as well as your outcome. Your list of standards is basically your list of what you deserve. Any time you accept anything less than what is on your new list of standards, you are saying you are not worthy.

You need only concern yourself with your standards. Don't worry about his standards. If you stick to your standards, your man will either come up to them, or he won't. If he doesn't, this clearly isn't the guy for you!

A standard is not to be confused with a wish list. Lists that you've made of "your perfect man" are not realistic. You never know who your soul mate is going to be, what he'll be doing for a living, or what he will look like, so don't limit yourself. As long as you are being true to your self—in other words, your standards and boundaries are adhered to—you will always attract the best possible man for you.

Please burn all of your lists, as true love doesn't require a list. You will know when you meet him if this is the guy for you, not because he fits the requirements on your list, but because you've connected on a deeper level. Get rid of all expectations and start with a totally clean slate. With a list, he's already failed before you've even met him, before he's even said hello. When you limit your choices to a list, you put blinders on, and you run the risk of missing out on someone great.

You need to be complete before you meet your soul mate. You can't look to a man to complete you; that is way too much pressure. No one can complete you, but you!

What does that mean? It doesn't mean you need to be your thinnest and prettiest, with all the plastic surgery money can buy, or that you need to have a successful career, or any other external things women think they need to complete them. A complete woman is simply one who is okay with herself and doesn't need any externals, or any man, to make her feel good about who she is.

How does one go about being complete? With a set of high standards and strong boundaries, that's how.

If you want to be treated properly and respected by the man you're dating, it is imperative that you create a list of standards for yourself. Think about these standards long and hard, and know that once you write them down, you can add to the list but not subtract from it. Your list of standards is basically your list of what you deserve. Any time you accept anything less than your list of standards, you are saying you are not worthy. On the contrary, the man you are with should feel like the luckiest guy on the planet to have landed you. Write down your list of standards and stick to them.

YOUR LIST OF STANDARDS

1. I will not pursue men. I will let men pursue me. That includes not accepting phone numbers from guys. I will tell them, "I don't call men, men call me." Also, I only give my number to guys I'm actually interested in going out with. If I'm not interested in him, I don't waste his time or my time. I will politely decline.

2. No more booty calls. No more friends with benefits. I will not sleep with a man until I am in a committed relationship with him, and he's in a committed, monogamous relationship with me.

3. I will not date a man who doesn't properly date me. Meaning: He must ask me out at least one day in advance. I will not be considered an afterthought.

4. I will be honest and up-front with my feelings and be clear about what I'm looking for.

5. I won't accept crumbs. I am worthy and will not settle for less than I deserve.

Your turn....

1. _____

2._____

3._____

4._____

5._____

Read your List of Standards many times a day, so you are one with your Standards. I can't tell you how many times I've seen women throw their standards out the window when a man comes around, so take this seriously and never let that happen.

BOUNDARIES

Once you've come up with your list of standards, it's time to learn about having boundaries. Boundaries are a little different from standards. Getting a man to behave the way he should, with appropriate boundaries, is very much like training a child. Jo Frost, the Super Nanny I mentioned in the beginning, advises using a "naughty mat" as an effective way to help discipline and train children to be well-behaved. The naughty mat is a mat that children have to sit on when they've been naughty. While on the mat, they get to regroup and think about what they've done wrong.

I like to use the same technique as a way to shift and change behavior patterns in our men. Men have learned bad habits, and women have allowed them to maintain their bad habits. When a parent doesn't have clear and strong boundaries with their child, the child will not cooperate. Training even the most badly behaved children is possible when you are clear about the rules and boundaries and you force a child to abide by them. If they don't, there are consequences, and rules and consequences must consistently be enforced by the parent. Eventually, the children break, and begin to follow the rules. The same applies to men.

Most men want to "have their cake and eat it, too." If at first they don't succeed, they will try and try again. Hold firm to your boundaries. It's very much like training a baby to cry it out at bedtime. Once a baby figures out that you're not coming back in to coddle him or her, they have no choice but to go to sleep. Again, when children misbehave, they are put in a time-out or put on the naughty mat. They may try to come out repeatedly, but once they figure out that what they are doing is not getting them anywhere, they will come out and apologize, and they will understand why they were punished in the first place. They're forced to understand the cause and effect of the situation. Ditto with your men.

If you've been in a relationship or situation where you've allowed your man to get away with murder, you will need to use Super Nanny-like tactics to break him of his bad behavior. It may sound funny, but it's the truth. At the end of the day, he will know how to treat you right, and he will have a great respect for you. If he doesn't, this is *not* the guy for you! Clearly, if he can't come up to your standards and adhere to your boundaries, he must go. *No exceptions!*

I always hear people talk about guys being jerks and treating women badly. From what I've observed, only a fraction of the men out there are just bad men. I actually think the vast majority of men are good guys who just behave badly because we, as women, allow them to. If a guy is behaving badly, showing you no respect, if he's saying he is going to call and doesn't, if he's standing you up on dates, this is all unacceptable behavior that is happening *only* because you are allowing it to happen. You are giving the man all the power and leaving yourself in a completely vulnerable, weak, and disadvantaged position.

If you go on a date and he says he will call you the next day and he calls you two weeks later, you explain very nicely that this is not the kind of guy you want to date, and you don't go out with him again. Or you can ignore him, if you feel he doesn't deserve a response, and move on. If you never hear from him again, clearly this is not the guy for you—and look at what a great boundary and standard you've set for yourself. You still hold all the power.

If he apologizes and asks for a second chance, and you truly like him and want to go out with him, you can give him another chance—but make sure that from that moment on, he comes up to your standards. One more slip and you'll have to let him go. Clearly, not the guy for you!

Here are a few more examples of setting standards and boundaries from various clients of mine:

1. A mutual friend introduced Victoria to a chef she had worked with on occasion. The mutual friend didn't know the guy that well,

but thought he'd be a good match for Victoria. They met briefly and he asked her out to lunch for the following Monday. As an aside, Victoria is very attractive, and the chef made numerous comments about how excited he was to get to know her. He told her he'd call Monday to confirm a time and place. Monday rolled around, and no call. As she is a client of mine, I've trained her well to read the signs, to let him take the lead, and to never call or text first. She followed my rules. Finally, he called her at noon and told her his son had an emergency. Of course, this is understandable, as emergencies trump everything else. My client has kids and knows that these things happen. They continued to make tentative plans every day for that week and somewhere along the way, lunch got downgraded to coffee. Every day the chef would call at the last minute to let her know why he couldn't make it that day. After the second time this happened, I instructed my client to ignore all further attempts, as clearly this guy wasn't that interested and she deserved better. She was reluctant to shut it down that quickly. On paper he seemed like a perfect match for her, and she reminded me that good guys are hard to find, especially for divorcées with kids. So I humored her to prove my point. After going back and forth for almost two weeks, and still no coffee date, let alone lunch or dinner, she finally pulled the plug and told him in no uncertain terms to get lost. Of course the minute she took her power back and created a standard for herself and a boundary for him, he couldn't get enough of her. He was texting and calling her, begging her to forgive him and go out with him. But she'd had enough. He had shown his true stripes very clearly, and she recognized the red flag. If he couldn't even commit to a coffee date, imagine what a future with this guy would've held.

2. Here's a different situation, but also a set-up through a mutual friend. This time the guy was a lawyer. The first time he invited Tracey out, it was to meet him on a Friday after work. Friday came and went and no call. Again, as these are my clients, they are well-trained to never call the guy first and always wait to hear from him, even if they had a date planned that night. If a man is standing you up, this is a red flag, so pay attention. If, God forbid, something

---

happened to him, which is the first place most women go when a guy doesn't call, you'll find out about it one way or another, but you don't need to call him. Anyway, the next time he contacted Tracey to ask her out, she stuck to her standard and called him out on standing her up. He apologized profusely, saying it was a misunderstanding and invited her to meet him for drinks the following night. Wanting to give him the benefit of the doubt, she agreed. Unbeknownst to her, when she showed up for what she thought was their "date," he'd brought his roommate along as well. She had no idea it was a group date! Even though they had a fun group date, the guy just didn't get it. He continued to text her for the next couple of weeks without making a formal plan or date. Tracey knew she was better than that, stopped responding to his texts, and let this one go. About a month later, he had his roommate send her messages through Facebook asking where she'd been and suggesting she go hang out with them. I guess if this were junior high, this kind of behavior would be acceptable, but this guy was a lawyer in his late thirties, and luckily Tracey was no longer desperate.

3. Laura came to see me after dating a man on-and-off for a year. This man broke her heart many times in that year, but he continued to come back to her, and she would take him back each and every time. She was absolutely convinced this man was her soul mate and felt he still just had some growing up to do. She had done many things right from the get-go. She waited months before having sex with him, she wasn't always available to him, she never contacted him but let him contact her, and she allowed him to chase and court her. Unfortunately, even after all of that, he was still scared to death of having a committed relationship, so he'd run away repeatedly. At first she blamed him for being disrespectful, but she came to realize through Girlfriend 911 that it was all *her fault*. She was the one allowing him to be disrespectful to her. She owned it! As a result, she sent him a powerful letter. Her letter is a great example of how empowering it is to have appropriate standards and boundaries. The minute she wrote this letter, the whole dynamic of her relationship changed for the better and the

balance of power shifted to her:

Jeff,

I want to explain why I haven't been responding to your messages. Simply put, I was taking the time to explore what I want and need in my life. This took some honest soul searching. I'm in a very different place than I was a year ago.

It's not my responsibility to tell you how women should be treated. It is, however, my responsibility to tell you how I demand to be treated. In fact, this isn't about you at all (I know this sounds cliché), but it's about my own expectations and my need to be respected.

When we met, you were a complete gentleman. You knew what a "proper date" was. You dated me for two months and then told me you weren't going to date other women, but I now know you were lying to get me to sleep with you. Everything changed after I did. That's when I began letting myself down by allowing you to cancel dates, leave me hanging, push me away, dump me, come back around, and ask for my company ONLY in the 11th hour. I don't feel like a lady whatsoever after all of this. These things are not acceptable to me, yet I've tolerated them simply to have you around, but I can't do that anymore.

I realize I'm entirely to blame for allowing you to repeatedly do things which hurt me. Hurt me once, shame on you. Hurt me twice, shame on me. The first time that I let you off the hook, I set a very bad precedent. That gave you license to repeat the same behavior, and I can't blame you.

You've made it quite clear to me over the past two weeks that you aren't interested in me for anything other than a booty call right now, but that's not ME at all. If I ever led you to believe that that's who I am, then I am embarrassed by my actions. I've represented myself poorly and untruthfully. The last few weeks have been invaluable in terms of the way I look at people, you included. I judge no one. I don't know your journey. I can only decide who I want in my life, while they make choices in their own lives. **If their choices don't support who I am, I have to be willing and able to let them go, but reserve the right to let them back into my life when and if their choices ever change.**

Laura

Since receiving her letter, Jeff got the message loud and clear. He's been working hard to come up to her standards. Laura changed how she behaved, so he is changing how he behaves. He no longer expects her to be a booty call, or breaks plans that he makes with her. They are happily dating, taking one step at a time, and moving forward in the right direction.

CHAPTER 6

READ THE SIGNS, GIRLFRIEND

Nothing is more important than learning how to read between the lines and not believing everything a man is telling you. If something *feels* off—it is. Your own gut is the finest lie-detector in the entire world. Keep *feeling* into yourself for the answers. *Do not allow anyone else in the entire universe to talk you into what you instinctively know is wrong for you.* Pay attention to his actions, not just his words.

I'm a big believer that signs are part of our everyday lives. A *sign* is defined as any action, event, or pattern that conveys a meaning. Pay attention to those signs. You really need to stop and figure out what they are telling you. Many of the signs given to us in relationships are *red flags*. A red flag is best described as a warning of danger or a problem. In relationships, red flags tell us when our man is not as interested in us as we'd like, or that he's not interested in monogamy. God forbid, the sign might be telling us the guy is actually married, or has a violent streak, so don't ignore them. A lot of you reading this book right now can probably think of many signs you've been given but chose to ignore. Signs are a road map to guide you and help you figure out what's really going on when your man isn't communicating. Signs inundate us in order for us to make the best decision about what to do next. The real art is figuring out how to recognize and read them. *Trust your gut—and stay out of your head!*

When you do see signs, especially if they are red flags, understand what they are telling you and act accordingly. Don't do the opposite in an attempt to make it all better, especially if the signs are clearly telling you to get out of the relationship. Ignoring glaring signs, when you know what they are telling you, is completely fear-based and can only and always lead to a much worse situation than you are presently in. Remember, however bad a situation is, it's the cover-up that truly leads to hell. Facing the truth and dealing with it will always bring relief. The truth heals.

A great example of this was when a famous politician's wife decided to renew her wedding vows shortly after learning her husband was having an affair. This is a clear example of ignoring one's gut (*i.e.*, your True Self) and doing the opposite in an attempt to make it better. Band-aids don't work, and eventually the problems get bigger. In this case, the politician's mistress got pregnant, and the whole sordid mess blew up very publicly.

One of the great things about men is that they are actually very simple creatures. Nothing about them is complicated. They may not be the best communicators, but they will give you all the signs you need. If you pay close attention not only to their words but to their actions, you will be able to figure out exactly what it is they want you to know but can't say. Since most men aren't comfortable opening up, it's our job to look for the clues. When you are in the dating phase, or the early stages of a relationship, the best way to gauge where your man is and how he feels about you is to always let him make the first move.

One of the biggest relationship signs to me is the issue of those three little words, "I love you." Whenever a relationship gets to the point where things have gotten very serious and he should say those words but doesn't, you need to pay attention. That's a clear sign that your man is either not ready or really not into you.

As I discuss in a later chapter about relationship Do's and Don'ts, the man must *always* say "I love you" first. By letting him say "I love you" first, you are getting a very clear sign as to where he is in the relationship. If you are at a point where he should be saying it, and isn't, that's a sign that you need to give him the time and space he needs to come to that conclusion, or face the fact that he's just not feeling it. Either way, when a man's not saying it well into a relationship, there's a problem. I know that's not what you want to hear, but it's the truth.

The mistake most women make in the beginning of a relationship is that they notice a sign, they know it's a red flag, but they totally *ignore it*. Many women refuse to acknowledge these glaring signs because they so desperately want to make it work and because they are operating out of total and absolute *fear*: fear of losing him and fear of being alone again. If it's a big red flag, and his behavior is unacceptable, then you have to *let him go*. If he's meant to be yours, he *will* come back to you, and if he's not meant to be yours, you've saved yourself a lot of time, energy, and pain.

Just to make it extra clear, I'm going to give you some examples of red flags and signs. These are actual incidents, true stories, about women and the signs that were clearly presented to them that they chose to ignore. I'm sure many of you have dealt with some of the exact same scenarios and will recognize some of these red flags. It doesn't mean you're an idiot if you've ignored them, but it does mean you need to learn from past mistakes and not repeat these mistakes in the future.

One red flag example that stands out the most to me is a story that Jenny Sanford told in her autobiography. For those of you who don't know her story, she was married to Mark Sanford, the Governor of South Carolina. He cheated on her very publicly with an Argentinean woman whom he called his soul mate. As a result, after twenty years of marriage, Jenny Sanford filed for divorce and subsequently wrote a book about her experience.

In the book, she revealed that when they got married, Mark wanted to take the word "faithful" out of their marriage vows. Now if that doesn't spell out his intentions in glaring red flag form, I don't know what does. If she'd been a client of mine, I would have told her to run for the hills. Unfortunately, she learned her lesson the hard way.

Here are some examples of red flags that clients and girlfriends have shared with me. Hopefully you won't recognize some of your own behavior in these, but if you do, take note of the sign(s) you missed!

1. He never introduced me to any of his friends and never invited me to his house,

even after a year of on-and-off dating.

2. I lived an hour and a half away from my guy, in California. Then I moved to his city for a job. When I told him I was moving there, he told me he was thinking about moving to New York.

3. He finally invited me to go to a barbecue at one of his friend's, when we were on our way back from an overnight getaway. But he said, "you're more than welcome to go with me," not "I'd love for you to go with me." When we were five minutes from the exit to the barbecue, he decided he didn't want to go to the barbecue anymore and dropped me off at my car instead. I had an extra day to spend with him, and he didn't even give me that option.

4. I had no idea if the guy I was dating was on the same page as I was, or if he wanted a committed relationship like I did. We had never discussed our future together, as I didn't want to freak him out. Nevertheless, I slept with him for the first time, and after that he cancelled the very next date that he had planned to take me on two days later. I

can't even express the kind of pain I was in.

5. He offered to take me on a real date again when we rekindled our friendship after a short breakup. I had to meet him at the restaurant. Once I got there, he tried to cancel the date because he was tired from a fishing trip. I wasn't happy, so he downgraded dinner to at least a quick drink and appetizer in the bar. He promised to make it up to me with a nice dinner on Thursday, and he flaked.

6. After our first two months of proper dating, he stopped planning dates in advance. He would only call me the day that he wanted to see me. I was always an afterthought.

7. We had the "let's take it to the next level" talk, and were supposedly dating exclusively when I discovered his online dating profile was still active. I had proof of recent logins to Match.com, Jdate, eHarmony, etc. I ignored all of them and bought his excuses. Ultimately, the relationship didn't work out. I wish I would have ended it the minute that red flag presented itself. I could have saved myself a great deal of pain.

---

8. I met a guy at a restaurant. He asked me out on a date and we dated for a few months. In the beginning, he showed me a lot of interest. The first thing that started to go was the phone calls. I should have read the signs and walked away, but I hung on for dear life. One night he cancelled on me and said he was sick. Shockingly, I ran into him that same night at an art show! When he saw me, he grabbed me and kissed me, tongue and all. I think he didn't know what else to do. After that, I never heard from him again.

9. I was dating a guy who said he wanted me to be his girlfriend. We had sex, and then he decided he was done and asked me to give him his key back. Even before sleeping with him, he stopped calling me regularly, or he'd call me last minute and say, "You can come to this or that...if you want." He was already pulling away, and I knew it, but I slept with him anyway. Big mistake.

10. I met a man who came on to me like crazy. He went to Peru, where he emailed me constantly and told me how much he missed me. He called me, almost obsessively, when

he got back. We dated, and everything was fine. Then we went to visit his grandmother together. He was a total jerk to me the entire trip. He made me drive while he kicked back and read a book the whole time, hardly talking to me at all. He ignored me completely at his grandmother's. I made the mistake of sleeping with him, even though I saw the red flag. After that, he took me out for Valentine's Day and bought me an orchid, so I slept with him again. Then he stopped calling. Eventually he called me to tell me he couldn't date me anymore, with no further explanation. I was so mad at myself. I knew in my heart it wasn't right, and I should have ended it. Yet I continued to date him and sleep with him even though most of the time he behaved like a complete asshole.

11. I received a fax from a girlfriend of mine with a picture of the guy I was dating. It was a wedding announcement in the New York Post. I was in such denial, convincing myself there must be a simple explanation, as I still had a key to his house. I thought surely if he was engaged he would have asked for his key back. I dated him a while longer before I

asked him about it.

12. I was dating a guy who only asked me out for Tuesday night dates. It used to really bother me that he never asked me out on a Friday or Saturday night, but I was too afraid to ask him why. I came to find out that he reserved the weekends for other women he was dating even though we were getting pretty serious and sleeping together. That was a major red flag that I ignored. I married him and got divorced four years later. Clearly, I was never a priority. I just wish I had seen it at the time.

13. I'd been dating a guy for three months and I was really into him. He helped a friend of his host a New Year's Eve party and didn't invite me. He told me he wanted to keep his options open, and I stupidly accepted that. I spent New Year's Eve home, alone and miserable. Unfortunately, it took another few years of this kind of behavior before I finally realized I deserved better.

Signs don't always come as red flags. Often they can be very positive. A lot of my clients have told me about some amazing signs they've seen, almost as if the universe was telling them that their guy was thinking about them. For example, when you see his car everywhere you look, hear his name numerous times a day, hear songs on the radio that were *your* songs, etc., pay attention. These are not coincidences, but great positive signs.

Case in point, with my client, Kerri. She had been dating Michael on-and-off for three years. After much heartache, and always giving him the benefit of the doubt, Kerri knew it was time to end things when he refused to commit. She wrote Michael a Goodbye Letter (I address Goodbye Letters in depth in Chapter 9) and for three months didn't hear a word from him. One night, while she was working at her job as a hostess in a restaurant, she was going over the reservation book for that night and the following night. She saw two names in the book and almost fell over. She couldn't believe what she was seeing. The following night there was a reservation for a Michael Leftin, and underneath that a separate reservation for a Jessica Brown. Her guy's name was Michael Brown. She took a picture of the reservation book and sent it to me. What a great sign!! I told her I was sure she would be hearing from him soon. I had no idea it would be that soon. The following day he called her for the first time in three months. He asked if they could have dinner so they could talk. He told her he couldn't stop thinking about her and he needed some more time. She told him to take as much time as he needed. Needless to say, she was thrilled at the way things were progressing.

I've had a few clients tell me they've been inundated with positive signs that remind them of their guy, only to hear from him a few days later. These signs are designed to put a smile on your face and help you keep the faith. So believe it.

CHAPTER 7

DO'S AND DON'TS FOR EVERY GIRLFRIEND

Years ago, I saw an episode of "Friends" that had a profound effect on me and stuck in my mind. When I decided to write *Girlfriend 911*, I thought it would be a perfect illustration of the world we live in today. A world that women have created for themselves, where they have no boundaries, no self respect, no dignity, and no self-worth. It's no wonder they can't find Mr. Right, and over half the people who do get married end up divorced.

This is the episode where Phoebe asks Joey for advice, because the guy she is dating won't put out. Joey tells her, "If you want to know what the deal is, you are going to have to ask him." So she does!

PHOEBE: Well, I finally took your advice and asked him what was going on.

JOEY: And what did he say?

PHOEBE: He said that, um, he understands how sex can be like, a very emotional thing for a woman and he was just afraid that I was gonna get all, ya know, like, "oh, is he gonna call me the next day" and, ya know, "where is this going" and, ya know, blah-la-la-la-la. So he said he wanted to hold off until he was prepared to be really serious.

JOEY: Wow.

PHOEBE: Yeah, so I said, "OK, relax please, y'know, I mean, sex can be just about two people right there in the moment, y'know." If he wants to see me again he can call, and if not, that's fine, too. So after a looooot of talking...I convinced him.

JOEY: Let me get this straight. He got you to beg to sleep with him, he got you to say he never has to call you again, and he got you thinking this was a great idea.

PHOEBE: Um-hum.

JOEY: This man is my god.

This is a very funny scene that is sadly so true for so many women who are out there in the dating world. With Internet dating and social

---

76

networking sites, it seems to me there is so much more choice, especially for men. It is like shooting fish in a barrel. All these available women, all in one location, all looking for the same thing: Them! How much easier could it be? Unfortunately, the mistake many women make is to think that by sleeping with the guy on the first or second date, they will somehow have an advantage over all the other women. This couldn't be further from the truth, as a guy will almost always go after the woman who is the biggest challenge and has the most respect for herself.

Women deserve to go after what they want in all other aspects of life, but when it comes to relationships, they absolutely need to be pursued and chased by men, *not the other way around.* Men must take the lead when it comes to relationships. Once you are in a committed relationship, equality rules, but up until then, he needs to do all the courting and chasing.

DATING DO'S

DO: Set a standard for yourself and stick to it. Let your potential suitor know that you need to be courted. That includes being taken out on proper dates and being asked out in advance for that date, not at the last minute. If a man can't plan a day in advance, then you are an afterthought.

DO: Let the guy know, by your actions, that if he wants you, he is going to have to work very hard to get you. Always wait to be asked out, never do the asking. Always wait to be called, emailed, texted, etc. Never reach out to him first until you are a good few months into a serious relationship.

DO: Let the man take the lead. If you go out on a date and you don't hear from him, that's your sign that he's not interested. Don't convince yourself that there is any other reason he's not calling you, and don't try to find an excuse to reach out to him. Texting him to say you "got home safely" is just an excuse. If he is that worried about you, let him be the one to check in with you. Thank him for the lovely date (assuming you had a great time) when the date is over and you say goodbye to him. No texting or calling the next day or days later when you haven't heard from him to "thank him" again. If he had such a good time, let him reach out first. The best rule of thumb is to let him lead the way, and you follow. If he's not pursuing you, he's not interested in the way you need him to be, so stop wasting your time and move on.

DO: Respect yourself. Save sex for when you're truly connected and in a committed relationship. "Friends with benefits" is never an option in the Girlfriend 911 world, because no matter how women try to justify it, they always get hurt. If you're good enough to sleep with, then why aren't you good enough to be in a relationship with? You want to make sure he is someone you actually want a relationship with and that takes time. If you are serious about finding a loving partner and being in a long-term relationship, then you shouldn't be giving up the most precious thing you can be giving a guy. Save it for the one who is right for you.

If you started out giving it up and there's a break in your relationship, you may still have a chance to redeem yourself. The rule of thumb is that two to three months is a good amount of time to wait before you sleep with a guy. By that time, you've gotten to know each other, you are a better judge of his character, and you have a better idea of whether or not this is going somewhere. I know women can fall in love on the first date and can usually tell right then and there if this has potential to be a long-term relationship or not. Men, unfortunately, are not nearly as decisive or intuitive as women are, so it takes them a lot longer to fall in love and know for sure what they want. If they are having sex from very early on in the relationship, before they have had a chance to actually fall in love or get to know you, it ends up complicating everything and usually, more often than not, they don't end up committing.

On the flip side, a girlfriend of mine met a guy she was crazy about. She was also convinced he was her soul mate. She actually did the right thing and followed all my rules...well, almost. She allowed him to court her and she waited over two months to have sex with him. What she neglected to do was have "the conversation"—the one in which you discuss your feelings and both decide to take the relationship to the next level of committed monogamy. No conversation was had. She just assumed they were both moving forward together into something deeper and more committed. Never, ever, ever assume. These are tough conversations to have, but that's what grown-ups do. Face the fear. You need to spell it out for him and make sure you're both on the same page. He got to have his cake and eat it, too. Completely unacceptable.

DO: Have a conversation about the status of your relationship before you start sleeping with him. So many women make this mistake. You have to make sure, before you have sex for the first time with a man you're dating, that he's not dating anyone else; that he's taken himself off of Internet dating sites; that he's not sleeping with anyone else; and that he sees this moving forward as a long-term, committed relationship. If you are sleeping with him, he should want what you want. You should both be on the same page. If you're too scared to have the conversation, or you think you're going to freak him out, that's a *huge sign* that you're not ready to be sleeping with him. You should be totally comfortable with each other and completely emotionally connected before you take it to the physical. Remember, you hold all the power. If you have sex too early on, and you're not ready, you've given away your power. That is never a good position to be in.

When you are ready to have sex with him, he had better be spending the night, and you'd better know with certainty that you will hear from him again either that day or at least the next day.

My client, Amber, before she was a client, had sex with a guy she'd been dating. There was no conversation before they slept together, and afterwards she didn't hear from him for 12 days, at which point he ended things. She was devastated. This is absolutely unacceptable behavior. Clearly, she wasn't ready to sleep with him. They hadn't built enough of a foundation in their relationship to take it to the next level, so when they did, it totally fell apart.

You can do everything else, but no actual intercourse, until you both have the same expectation that you are going to be a couple and your relationship is moving in the right direction. When you have this crucial conversation, it takes all of the guesswork out of where he is emotionally, what he's thinking, and whether you're a couple or not. If he's not ready to make that kind of commitment, at least now you know where you stand.

The reason why I'm such a stickler for not jumping into bed when the first opportunity arises is because more often than not, sex does something very different for women than it does for men. When a man sleeps with you, he enters your body and his energy is literally inside of you. That energy stays with you. The same obviously isn't true for men, so, logically, you can see why women get emotionally attached so quickly, and it takes men a lot longer.

Holding off on having sex has become the running joke amongst my girlfriends. We called it "guarding your treasure," which evolved into "don't let him looty your booty!" So please, ladies, until all the pieces of the puzzle are in place, you know in your heart you are both ready, and the timing is perfect, don't rush into it. Better to just *wait, wait, wait.*

If your man has come back to you, it's still imperative that you don't sleep with him right away. He needs to earn your trust all over again. You need to have time to get to know each other again and make sure he's come back for the right reasons. I'm not telling you to wait another three months, but don't jump in the sack on the first date just because the passion and chemistry is so intense. When you can clearly see that he wants to be with you long-term, his words match his actions, and he behaves like a man, not a little boy, then it's time to make that decision. This could be a matter of weeks or months. You will know in your heart when the time is right.

Please don't give the "I couldn't help it" excuse, and "You don't understand, we couldn't keep our hands off each other." Of course I understand, but if you sleep with him too soon and you aren't getting the respect you want, remember *it's all your fault.* It's back on you and has nothing to do with him. How your guy shows you respect is all up to you. You control that. You have all the power, not the other way around.

DATING DON'TS

DON'T: Beg, plead, pressure, or guilt. Begging, pleading, and literally pushing a guy up against a wall and guilt-tripping him into being with you is very unattractive. Desperation equals turn-off. Independence and self-respect equal turn-on.

DON'T: Represent yourself poorly or cheaply. Don't text or email naked pictures of yourself. Less is more. Less boobs all over the place, less dressing like a hooker, less giving it all up on the first, second, or third date. You don't want to represent yourself as a floozy. Leave more to the imagination. It ends up being so much more attractive while you're still in the dating phase.

DON'T: Ever settle for being a mistress. These days, being a mistress seems to be a badge of honor. For some reason, we have put mistresses on a pedestal. This is hideous to me.

Affairs are never authentic and are never in truth, no matter how much you try to convince yourself they are. Why would anyone knowingly settle for being second best? It is so disempowering. Unless a man is separated, or no longer married, this should never be an option. You can't expect anyone to respect you if you don't respect yourself. If a man truly loves you, he needs to exit out of the situation, no exceptions.

DON'T: Try to make your man jealous. Women sometimes do pathetic things to try to get a man's attention. If he wanted to be with you, he'd be with you. Making your guy jealous can sometimes work in the short term, but long-term they realize why they ended it with you in the first place, and you just get hurt all over again.

One client of mine, before working with me, had arranged to have a male friend pose as her date at a party where she knew her man would be. A few too many drinks led her to get a little too risqué on the dance floor, and caused her to aggressively make out with her date in front of him. Her man was not impressed. In fact, he couldn't have cared less, and she felt like a complete idiot. Please do not play these childish games. They honestly don't work in the long run. You want this man to respect you, and ultimately to spend his life with you, right? So why would you think this behavior is acceptable?

DON'T: Start going places that you know your guy is going to be in the hopes of "bumping into him." That is you trying to control and manipulate the situation, and doesn't allow him the time he needs to figure out how he really feels about you.

DON'T: Be the first to say "I love you"—ever!—no matter how long you've been dating, or how right it seems in the moment. It has to come from him first! When guys say they love you, they mean it. So, if he hasn't said it, he's either not ready to say it, or his feelings aren't what they should be. Pay attention to that sign, because it's a big one! If you say it first, you will never know how he truly feels and whether he's saying it because he feels obligated and doesn't want it to be weird or awkward, or because he truly means it. Allowing the guy to do everything first is a great indicator of how he feels about you, and where he is in your relationship. These are huge signs that you need to pay attention to. Think of them as road maps for the journey ahead.

So many women are so eager to move forward in the relationship that they either miss the signs, or they ignore them completely. They get frustrated when the guy hasn't said he loves them, so they say it first, thinking that it will just speed things up. What they should do is stop and pay attention to what that sign really means.

DON'T: Buy a man a gift when he hasn't given you a gift first. Never buy him a gift until he has bought something for you. If you're celebrating birthdays and his comes first, again read the signs of the relationship and proceed cautiously. If you've been casually dating for three months, buying him dinner for his birthday is probably appropriate. Six months? Maybe dinner and a small gift, but no more. You be the judge, but be smart about it. Some women think the bigger and more expensive and lavish the gift, the more they will endear her to the guy, and the more he will love her. Unfortunately, it doesn't work that way. Too many gifts from a woman too early in a dating situation can be very overwhelming for a guy, and can be a complete turn-off.

I know so many women who put most of the effort into the relationship in an attempt to control everything. They literally will do almost anything to keep it together, especially if they start feeling he's not that into it. Instead of just letting things happen naturally and organically in the relationship, they are always the ones making the "plans" as a sort of fail-safe to keep him around. After all, we convince ourselves that if we have plans in place, our man isn't going anywhere.

If things aren't developing naturally, *read the signs*. This might not be the relationship for you. If he wants out, understand you have to let him go, and move on. Remember a very important point that a lot of women either can't accept or simply ignore: you can't make someone love you!

As I was writing this paragraph, a girlfriend of mine called to ask me a relationship question. A friend of hers had been in a new relationship for about three months, but things had been moving very quickly and they were actually heading for marriage. Anyway, he was going out of town for the weekend to Florida, to a bachelor party, and this girl decided to sit him down and explain to him her expectations for the weekend. Basically, she told him she needs the same attention that he gives her when he's in town, and that she expects him to call and text her with updates throughout the weekend. See what I am talking about here? Stop trying to control everything, especially him.

A better approach, and the one I would recommend, is for her to have said nothing whatsoever. She should've wished him well and then waited to see how it unfolded, organically. By that I mean that she should've waited to see if she heard from him or not, while he was away.

This is where the "read the signs" part of Girlfriend 911 comes into play. If he ended up calling her and texting her all weekend long, that would be a great sign that he missed her. Just because she was out of sight didn't mean she was out of mind. If, on the other hand, he had gone radio silent for the weekend, that would be a bad sign, and would need to be addressed once he returned. That would be what I would call a serious red flag. Probably not enough of a red flag to end the relationship, unless this was his way of telling her he wanted out, but enough to warrant a discussion about how not being in touch all weekend, when they were talking about getting married, was just not the kind of relationship she wanted to be in.

Some of this stuff might seem basic to a lot of

you, but I know a lot of women who have done far too many of the DON'TS at one time or another.

CHAPTER 8

IT'S ALL ABOUT TIMING, GIRLFRIEND

Before we begin the program, I need to talk about one more thing that is very important in helping women follow the steps of the program, and that is *timing*. Timing is everything!

It's true what they say: men and women really are from different planets. We are different in so many ways, including our timetables. As I'm sure you ladies have discovered, men are usually in no hurry to commit to a monogamous relationship, or to settle down. So it's very important that once you commit to doing "the program," you get rid of any kind of time constraints and understand that this process could take a day, a week, six months, five years, or maybe even more. Seriously, even if it takes several years, if this man is truly your soul mate, and the person you are going to spend the rest of your life with, then that period of time suddenly doesn't seem so long. Right? Stop thinking in terms of instant gratification and concentrate on the big picture!

Now I understand a lot of you are going to have a difficult time with this concept because you don't want to wait, you don't want to be alone, and your biological clock is ticking. But why would you want to settle down and have children with the wrong person, only to get divorced a few years later? Once you have children, it's even harder to get out. Unfortunately, I know many people who have found themselves in this situation, and it's almost always acrimonious, painful, and difficult. I really believe the better option is to wait for the right guy to come along. If you want to have children and feel you're running out of time, explore other options, like adoption, sperm banks, or freezing your eggs.

"Guy Time" is what I like to call the time men take to process and figure things out. The problem with Guy Time is it almost always takes a much longer time than any of us women want to wait. Men need to consider many factors when deciding whether or not you are the one for them. They need time to process the relationship, to really figure out how they feel, and to see what their life would be like without you. Often men have to do work on themselves first, before they feel ready to take the next step with you. So with Guy Time, it will take as long as it takes. You have to respect that and surrender to this process.

Men do not typically fall in love as fast as women do. It's just the way it is. If they do fall in love, they may not be willing to face it or do anything about it for a very long time. Understand this and get used to it. It can be a bitter pill to have to swallow when you know you are in love with a man, and he cannot reciprocate or share his feelings. Remember, you can't force someone to love you. He has to get there on his own. If there is absolutely no chance for the two of you, and never was, you will know that as well, and you will be able to heal your heart quickly and move on with your life.

When a man is finally ready to spend the rest of his life with you, he will be knocking down your door. He will want to shout your name from the rooftops. He will move heaven and earth, but it's not going to happen overnight, so hold your horses and be patient. By doing my program, you will start to see fairly quickly the signs and signals he is sending you. That will help you to move in the right direction and continue on with the program.

In most cases, women are correct when it comes to matters of the heart. Women are naturally intuitive, especially when they feel they've finally met the love of their life. But that doesn't mean that the man will recognize it right away himself. Give it time. Even if he feels it, it will most likely scare him to death. As I mentioned before, this is a typical time for men to run, so please don't let it destroy you. Be strong and stay true to your self. If it's real, he will come back. You probably know the old saying, "If you love something, set it free. If it comes back, it's yours. If it doesn't, it never was."

SECTION 2
MY PROVEN PROGRAM

STEP 1

THE GOODBYE LETTER

You are about to embark on the Girlfriend 911 program. This section was originally designed for women in unfulfilling, unhappy relationships or for women who want to be in a committed relationship but end up dating men who are not on the same page. But single women can benefit from this section as much as those in a relationship; recognizing unhealthy dating habits and learning how not to repeat those patterns in future relationships is universal. So if you're single, keep reading!

The first step in my program is to take back your power and put yourself in the driver's seat. This is done by stating your truth in what I call your "Goodbye Letter." This is not necessarily a goodbye to your man, but instead a goodbye to the old way of doing things. You are putting him on notice that the way the relationship has been up until now ceases to exist. Things are going to be different.

This step is non-negotiable. It's the critical first step on the path to turning things around. You are going to lay all of your cards on the table, and then you are going to walk away. You are going to state very clearly how you feel about the guy and what you want out of the relationship, and then you are going to let him know that if he's not on the same page, you're going to be moving forward without him. This may be one of the hardest things in the world to do, but it has to be done.

The Goodbye Letter is always written, and preferably sent via email. I've had many clients argue with me that they'd rather do it face-to-face, or on the phone, as sending an email seems cold and impersonal. The reason I always insist that it's done in a letter form is so that it is written in stone. Your thoughts are clear and concise, he can keep it forever, and it allows him to read it over and over again and to really get the full effect of what you're saying. If this is done any other way, the words are easily forgotten and the message is lost, and you run the risk of not saying everything you want to say.

Without fail, every client I have worked with

who sends a Goodbye Letter receives a similar response. It's uncanny. Basically, the guy says he's not on the same page and does not see a future relationship. I counsel all of my clients to expect this response because, let's face it, if their guys were ready to be in a long-term, committed relationship, these women wouldn't need my help and wouldn't be writing this letter in the first place.

I can't tell you how many of my clients are devastated when they receive these responses. I always tell them to just wait and see what he does after that initial Goodbye Letter. His actions are the true indicator of how he feels. The way all these men respond to the Goodbye Letters is the perfect example of what I described in an earlier chapter as Opposite Day. They *all* say they don't want to be in a relationship with said client—and yet when my client explains that if they make that choice they can no longer be in her life, I've yet to see one guy who has run for the hills, never to be heard from again. In other words, they say one thing and *do* another. They all ignore the part of the letter that says, "I cannot be friends with you, and you cannot be in my life," and they always reach out in one form or another.

This, I tell my clients, is the fun part. This is when you get to see how they truly feel about you.

For a lot of women, writing this letter is a

terrifying experience. You're laying your true feelings out there, you're exposed and vulnerable. But I've learned from my own experience that when you are in a situation with a guy you have history with—in other words, you've been on and off for years and are not getting what you want, or you're in a relationship and not getting what you want—laying all of your cards on the table is the only way to take control of the situation, take back your power, and once and for all find out from his actions, not his words, how he truly feels about you.

EXIT GRACEFULLY

After sending your Goodbye Letter, "Exiting Gracefully" is the next most important thing you can do in this process. Unfortunately, women typically do the opposite of what they should do. When a guy is pulling away, they tend to lunge toward him. They get desperate, needy, clingy, and do whatever it takes to try to keep him. It is incredibly unattractive to the person who is trying to break away, or just needs some space. If you really don't want to lose him, the trick is to do the opposite of what you instinctively want to do. If he is pulling away you need to *pull away as well.* If he wants to come back, he has to do it on his own terms, because he wants to, not because you forced him or guilted him into being with you.

Once you've sent the Goodbye Letter, you will probably be sick to your stomach. As I've said before, this is not for the faint of heart. It's a very difficult process, but it's well worth it. In Chapter 9, "What Now?", I'll give you all the tools you'll need to move forward smoothly, easily, and in the right direction. So stay strong, stay focused, and keep your eye on the big picture!

When you Exit Gracefully, you give the person time and space to think about what he wants. He may realize he's making a big mistake, but if you don't Exit Gracefully, you blow that chance. If it turns out the relationship is over, you get to walk away with pride and dignity without feeling bad about yourself. Women who are constantly behaving badly (no boundaries, no self-respect) feel awful about themselves. If you take control of the situation and take your power back, even if you don't get the outcome you'd hoped for, just being true to your self, and having appropriate standards and boundaries, will make you feel great about yourself. When you practice this, it really works. Exiting Gracefully is one of the most empowering things you can do.

You can't guilt a man into loving you. When I

was in my twenties I had a girlfriend who was three years into a relationship that she thought was heading towards marriage. By all accounts they had a great relationship, and the future seemed bright. One day, out of the blue, her boyfriend told her she wasn't the one and he just didn't see them moving forward. He knew in his heart he didn't want to marry her, and he was honest about it. Of course there had been a few red flags along the way, but she had ignored them.

I wish I had known then what I know now. I would have put her on the program and maybe the outcome would have been different. Instead, however, I listened to what she told me and offered no advice. She said they'd had a long talk and she had managed to convince him that he had made a mistake, and so they weren't breaking up after all.

You can't convince anyone, and why would you want to? If he made a mistake by leaving her, he had to come to that conclusion on his own. He had to be the one to realize he made the mistake; she couldn't tell him.

Needless to say, six months later when my friend's boyfriend plucked up the courage again, he did manage to end things. In her desperation to change his mind and make him see what he was missing, she kept sleeping with him, no strings attached. She had no respect for herself, so he had no respect for her. She didn't Exit Gracefully; instead, she clung on for dear life. As a result, it didn't end well, and she was left completely and utterly devastated.

Please understand, you can't beg and you can't plead and you most certainly can't throw yourself on the ground and carry on like a pathetic little girl. If someone is expressing their honest feelings, you have to respect their wishes and let them go. It's not for you to decide for him. No drama. No histrionics. No sobbing. No cyber-stalking (Facebook, MySpace, Twitter, etc.). No drive-bys. No texts. No phone calls. No guilt. No using sex, or sexual favors. Just leave! If they come to a different conclusion, without any input from you, then that is the clearest and most definitive sign that they truly want to be with you.

Of course it's natural to miss your man after you've exited, and the longer it takes to hear from him, the harder it is to wait, but you have to be at peace with it. You are starting with a blank canvas. You have no idea what the future holds. He may or may not come back to you permanently. You have to get on with your life in the meantime and see what unfolds.

One of my clients, Danielle, came to me because her boyfriend got cold feet and abruptly ended their five-month relationship. He was newly divorced and afraid of messing up another long-term relationship. Danielle was devastated, so she wrote him a Goodbye Letter, told him how she felt about him, and what she wanted in terms of a future together.

He told her he couldn't do it. Of course he tried to persuade her to continue to be in his life on a casual basis with "no strings attached," but this was not an option for her. She cut off all communication with him and got on with her life. Six months later he came back, and two years later they got married. She set high standards and boundaries for herself. She trusted her instincts in knowing this was the man for her, and waited it out. She also followed every one of my rules, and it paid off big time.

Another one of my clients, Cheryl, met a guy that she was crazy about. For five years they had an on-and-off, very passionate, very sexual, and also very tumultuous relationship. Bottom line, she wanted to be in a monogamous, long-term relationship, and he didn't. They had amazing chemistry, the sex was great, they always had fun when they were together, and he had expressed on many occasions that he loved her, but he just couldn't make the commitment that she desperately wanted him to make. He was younger than she was and felt he couldn't provide for her and her two children. She worked and didn't think this should be an issue.

Before she came to see me, she'd spent three years trying to convince him, begging and pleading at times, to make the commitment. The more he rejected her, the more desperate and needy she got, settling for far less than she deserved and having absolutely no standards or boundaries. She would be at his beck and call whenever he decided to come around, and at times would sleep with him with no strings attached just to have him in her life.

Accepting "crumbs" in this case is an understatement. It was time to exit. When Cheryl came to me, I told her she clearly had no respect for herself, and as a result he had no respect for her either. I told her she'd have to send him a Goodbye Letter stating exactly what she wanted from him, and then she'd have to wait and see what he did. It was imperative that she exit gracefully from the situation. She followed my program, and although he told her he wasn't on the same page, he's still contacting her to this day, slowly but surely coming up to her new standards.

Another client, Melissa, was in an on-and-off four-year relationship with Jake, who just couldn't commit. The first few months were blissful, but when Jake started realizing that Melissa wanted to get serious, he started to pull back. A game of cat-and-mouse ensued. They would get together, then break up, then she'd beg and plead for him to come back, suggesting at times that they "just hook up" or be each other's "booty call" in a desperate attempt to see him under any circumstances. He would cancel on her all the time, not return texts and calls, and tell her over and over again that it wasn't going to work out for them. Yet three years later, he was still in her life.

Something had to be done. Her situation was causing her so much pain and anxiety, she couldn't sleep, was having a hard time functioning at work, and had been on an emotional roller coaster for way too long. It was controlling her life. It was clear to me that she needed to take her power back, and she needed to set some standards and boundaries for herself and her guy. So we did Step One of the program and wrote him the following Goodbye Letter:

Dear Jake,

I just read something recently that really resonated with me. It's called the "single bullet theory." Basically, the theory goes that everyone has one person out there. One bullet. If you're lucky in life, you

get to meet that person. And once you do, you're shot through the heart, then there's nobody else. No matter what happens, no one else can ever come close.

There is no doubt in my mind that you, Jake, are that person for me. No matter what you say, or what you believe, or how you try to push me away, once I met you there was no one else who ever came close or who ever made me feel the way you do. That being said, it doesn't seem fair to me that just when things get so great between us you always pull away with no explanation, shut me out, and then it's over, until the whole cycle starts again. This last time has been particularly tough and devastating for me, and I've realized for my own emotional well-being, I just can't do this anymore. I told you before I have been working very hard on myself this past year trying to break old patterns and not live in that "bubble." If you reread all my emails since January you should know beyond a shadow of a doubt how I feel about you and where I stand. If you

dig deep down in your heart and your soul I hope you can be very honest with yourself as to exactly what it is that you want. If it's not me and you don't have the same feelings that I do then please let me go.

Melissa.

Although Melissa was petrified after sending this letter, she felt a great calm come over her as she realized for the first time in four years, she was in control of the situation, and no matter what the outcome, she instinctively knew she'd be okay. She exited truthfully, gracefully, and with her dignity intact, and those three things empowered her.

Another example of a great Goodbye Letter came from my client Julia. She was a friend of another client of mine, and had found herself in a rather unusual situation. She was a year into a relationship with her boyfriend, Dave. She thought they had a great relationship. She was deeply in love with him and was hoping they would get married in the near future. Both had been married before and had children.

Unfortunately, she and Dave were not on the same page. Although he wanted to continue dating her, he also wanted them to explore the "swinging lifestyle" and invite other couples into their relationship.

Julia was terrified of losing him. She truly believed he was her soul mate, but every time she thought about him sleeping with other women, she got sick to her stomach. She was very conflicted when she came to see me, and I immediately told her to write down her list of standards and boundaries. When she could clearly see that the list didn't include sex with other women, she knew she had no choice but to exit the relationship gracefully and on her terms. If he came back, then he'd made the decision to be with her and only her. If he didn't, then at least she had her self-respect and dignity intact.

Julia received the following email from Dave, which prompted her to send her Goodbye Letter:

Julia,

I couldn't sleep at all last night and can't now either. Just racing thoughts about you and me. Replaying a bunch of memories (good ones!) over and over again. No matter how hard I try, honey, I can't stop seeing the images of all our wonderful times together.

Why do I feel so sad, and why does it

feel like we broke up?.....that's not what is going on for me but I think maybe you think I'm just trying to break us up slowly.

I miss you and love you! and....I always will. And I am so grateful that you came into my life!...and are in it. I want to be with you again, and keep having fun with you!... and make love to you! Do you feel the same at all?

I don't want you to leave being in my life....but if certain future dreams and hopes have been shattered for you by me and you need to be apart from me now or to sort that out..... I understand.

How do you feel about tomorrow?....Can we be together....do you even want to?

I want to. I want to hold you again.

Love,
Dave

Julia's response (Goodbye Letter):

Dave,

Thanks for your email. I am really glad that you sent it cause I have been thinking a lot as well and wanted to take the time to write down my thoughts and express to you how I feel and where I am at.

Since our conversation at the park, I've done a lot of thinking about what we discussed. Like you, I am also very sad. I don't think that you are trying to break us up slowly, but I do think that you want me in your life and you also want to date and sleep with other women and this, Dave, definitely does not work for me. To be honest, I don't understand the lifestyle that you seek and it's hard for me to imagine myself staying in a relationship with someone who feels he needs to share his love with multiple women.

I'm sorry that you felt you have lost your social life and things were no longer fun for you. I totally respect the fact that you have been honest with me about your

111

wants and needs, so I need to be honest with you—this is not something I can be a part of. I would be so miserable knowing that you were with other women. I would love to think I could casually date you, but the truth is, I can't. I want to be with you in a monogamous, committed relationship and if that is not where you are at, then I do think at this point it is best that we go our separate ways.

Dave, I hope you know this is a very difficult decision for me, and I sincerely wish things could be different as I am absolutely in love with you. We have shared so many amazing times together over the past year. And, of course, our incredible sexual connection will be hard for me to ever forget. I also wanted you to know that no one has made me feel the way you do when we are together. I feel truly blessed that I was able to have you in my life.

Love,
Julia

We will come back to the outcome of these stories later in my "If He Reaches Out" chapter, but for now I want to give you a few more Goodbye Letter examples.

It's never too late to start the Girlfriend 911 program, write a Goodbye Letter, and create standards and boundaries for yourself, even if up until now you've done *everything wrong*.

Case in point: my client Tiffany. Tiffany wasn't in a relationship, or even in a situation with her guy, when I advised her to write a Goodbye Letter. She had been on three dates with a man she was really into and slept with him every time. What's worse, when he wasn't contacting her for any further dates, she sent him a text asking if it would be okay for them to use each other as booty calls.

Now, what man is going to turn that down? How on earth could this guy ever have any respect for Tiffany? Of course he did call her for a booty call, but only once. He went silent for long periods of time in between. Months later, he reached out to her on Facebook just to check in, and she wrote back asking him if they could get together sometime. He never responded.

Tiffany was in such a dark place and feeling so terrible about herself and the situation that her friend recommended she contact me immediately. I wanted her to Exit Gracefully with standards and boundaries, but she couldn't just send a goodbye email out of the blue, or he would've thought she was crazy. This is the first client I'd worked with who didn't have years or at least months of history with the guy. It had just been three dates.

We needed to do something to get a reaction out of him so that she could reply to his response with a Goodbye Letter. I advised her to delete him from Facebook. I told her that after deleting him, if she never heard from him again, that was a clear sign that he had absolutely no interest, and she needed to let him go and move on. However, if he noticed that she deleted him and responded, she had hope of salvaging this situation and starting afresh using the Girlfriend 911 program.

Of course she argued with me. She didn't want to delete him from Facebook, as she was reluctant to lose the only connection she had to him. I can't force someone to do something they don't want to do, so I told her to think about it and call me in a few days time.

She called me three days later and told me she was very depressed. I explained again that I thought she should delete him from Facebook. That was the next step. She finally complied and less than 24 hours later, he sent her a text asking what she was doing that night. This was the perfect opportunity to write her Goodbye Letter, and this is what she sent:

> **Hey Paul,**
>
> **I got your text this morning, it was good to hear from you. Not sure if you were looking to make plans, but thought this might be a good time to let you know where I'm at.**
>
> **I've done a lot of thinking lately in regards to my dating situation, and what I'm really looking for is a committed relationship. I realize our arrangement in the past has been casual, but I think you're a great guy, and I've had such fun hanging out with you that I would like to take it to the next level. I understand if you're not on the same page, but I wanted to be clear about what I'm looking for.**
>
> **Tiffany**

Surprisingly (considering there was no real history), he sent her back this lovely reply:

> **I totally understand. I hope you are well,**

too. I wish you the best with your living situation, etc. Take care, Green Eyes...

There are two signs to pay attention to in his response. First, he called her "Green Eyes," which was a flirty term of endearment he'd used on their first two dates eight months earlier, and had not used since. And second, he signed off with an ellipsis (...) which always means unfinished business to be continued.

I told her she would hear from him again, and she did. Paul reached out a few more times, asking if Tiffany would like to grab a drink, but the timing was never right. The last text was sent to her a couple of hours before he wanted to grab the drink. Adhering one hundred percent to the Girlfriend 911 program, with strict standards and boundaries now fully intact, this is what she sent:

> **Hi, it's nice to hear from you. I would really love to see you, but a last minute drink seems like an afterthought. Our old pattern was not healthy for me. I hope you understand.**

Here's his reply:

> **Yes, I do. I am just in a funk and would**

have loved to chat and be around your gentle energy. I apologize for my insensitivity I showed you in the past.

For a situation that looked like nothing to begin with, it certainly hasn't turned out that way. "I apologize for my insensitivity I showed you in the past." Now that's the kind of reaction we're looking for.

It took another couple of months before Paul completely changed his tune. He couldn't stop thinking about Tiffany and what it would mean to live without her. He found her new high standard very attractive. He reached out again, finally asking her out on a proper date, and they've been together ever since. Two months into the relationship, he asked her what kind of ring she wanted and told her entire family how much he loved her.

My second case in point of why it's never too late to get yourself on the program is my client Rebecca. Rebecca had been involved in a 10-year "friends with benefits/booty call" situation. They were good friends who hung out and did a lot of stuff together, but also had sex whenever he wanted it, with no strings attached. She was in love with him and couldn't get him to commit to a real relationship. At times, however, there seemed to be glimmers of hope, especially when he started talking about them having a child together.

Unfortunately, his behavior was Opposite Day personified. He would say one thing, and do another. Needless to say, she was a complete mess. After ten years of this, I advised her enough was enough. Clearly, her way wasn't working. It was time to do it the Girlfriend 911 way. Below is her Goodbye Letter:

Dear Sam,

I have been thinking for a while now about writing down my thoughts and feelings where you are concerned, in the hopes that I might be able to get some clarity as to exactly what we are doing. Although initially my first choice would be to have a face-to-face conversation with you, after much thought I realized a letter might be a better plan, as it will give me a chance to be really clear with you in terms of what I want to say, and it will give you a chance to really think about what I am saying.

I guess the gist of this letter is that I am incredibly confused as to exactly what it is that you want from me. It was not

long ago that you sat me down and told me straight out that you wanted to buy a house with me and have a baby. I know our relationship has been very rocky over the years with many ups and downs, but that conversation gave me the impression you were ready to settle down with me. It has felt to me like you have been pursuing me for a long time now and the impression you have given me is that you want to be with me not just as a casual lover, but as a life partner. Having a baby together is not something I take lightly. I have no interest in being a single mom, so when you said you want to have a baby with me I took you at your word, as I couldn't imagine anyone would joke about something like that. I guess the next logical step to me after a conversation like that was that our relationship would move to the next level. The level of planning to be together in a loving and stable relationship and planning to be parents. The problem is, Sam, that except for continuing to have very casual sex with me whenever it suits you, nothing has really changed, and in fact, in my mind, our relationship has regressed rather than progressed.

Please understand this letter is not about me being mad at you, but more me trying to understand your point of view and letting you know mine. You seem to say one thing and yet your actions are completely different. I am not sure if you realize, but I have been trying to see you for 3 weeks now and you just never seem to be available. I know you are very busy at the moment with your job, but if we were seriously considering having a child, this would be very worrisome for me. You said last month that sometimes I just have to wait for you to get over it, so that's what I've been doing. I'm not screaming or making demands, and I don't want to get into a fight with you, but I want you to know that I really would love to work this out, but it is extremely frustrating for me when you make little effort, I don't see you for weeks on end, weekends come and go with no calls and no hanging out. At this point, "I didn't have time to call" doesn't work as an excuse for me. In this day and age with cell phones, and email, and text messaging, it takes no more than 15 seconds to say I'm running late or it's just not going to happen today.

I totally understand that during the work week you are working so many hours and it's intense, but if you are serious about being in a relationship with me it should be a priority to find time to spend together. It seems to me that over the last month you have not wanted to see me. For example, you invited me for dinner and you showed up two hours late. It was very distressing to me that you didn't even bother to call or send me a text letting me know that you were going to be so late. When you do finally show up, we have incredible (in my opinion) babymaking sex, you leave my bed, kiss me goodbye, and I don't hear from you again for over a week. It is so hurtful to me, Sam, and I just don't understand it. It definitely makes me feel like the baby thing was just lip service and is not your true intentions. After all, you haven't even bothered to ask me over these past couple of months if I am pregnant!

Just so we are clear, Sam, I do want the whole package and I want it with you: a relationship, mutual commitment, consistency and respect, and God willing, a beautiful, healthy child. I know we have the love already, but I need to know whether this is something you are serious about, because from your actions these past few months it doesn't seem like it to me. I hope you will take the time to really think things through and be very honest with me and yourself as to exactly what it is that you want, and how we should move forward, whether it is together or apart.

Rebecca

Sam replied with the following:

Hi Rebecca,

I'm sorry for not replying to your email earlier, but I deleted it, accidentally, from my Blackberry and could not find it on my computer, so never actually got to read it completely!

I remember our conversation where I told you of my feelings for you, and in some part they are still there, but as I imagine you have noticed, not as strong as they were then. I guess my biggest fear with regard to a relationship with us is the volatility that exists between us, and how we seem to see-saw from friends to enemies so swiftly. Obviously I am to blame in no small part for some of these rifts that have occurred, but I have come to think that if as "friends" we can be so up and down, how could we survive as a partnership?

Our recent forays back into bed with each other have, as always, been fantastic, but I became scared that I was getting into a situation that we may both regret, namely falling into a relationship that could, ultimately, end up being an unhappy one for both of us. I don't know that for sure of course, but it was a genuine concern. I am sorry for being elusive over the last few weeks, and as you rightly point out, not taking the responsibility of checking up on you, particularly considering the risk of pregnancy. I sincerely apologize for that! I imagine that you are not pregnant, or I would have heard from you, but maybe I am wrong. If so, please tell me!

I don't want you to think that I had not called simply because I wanted to avoid you that really is not the case. As I told you, I have had some torrid weeks of late, and that has fed into the problem. I know you probably think I am a maniac and have been possessed, but exhaustion would be nearer the truth. This has been compounded by discovering on Monday that I am the victim of identity fraud and someone has racked up credit card bills in my name to the tune of $78,000.

C'est la vie!! Do you want to meet for coffee on Saturday and we can talk? Yes, I said coffee.

Sam XX

There would be no meeting for coffee, as Rebecca had already said everything she needed to say, but the fact that Sam signed off his letter with two kisses told me everything I needed to know. Reading between the lines, I knew he'd be back. It took some time, but he started reaching out every few months or so, desperately trying to get back to the way things were. Rebecca stayed true to her new set of standards and boundaries, and using the "Personal Mantra" (to be discussed in more detail in a later chapter), she told him every time he got in touch with her that he wasn't allowed back in her life until he was ready to be in it full-time.

Two years later, he called to say he was ready for that proper relationship. Ten years doing it her way, and two years doing it the Girlfriend 911 way, she finally got what she had always wanted.

STEP 2

SURRENDER TO THE PROCESS

The most important thing you can do after step one, The Goodbye Letter, is step two: *Surrender.* You must surrender to how this whole thing plays out, without any attachment to the outcome. For those of you who don't know what surrendering is (yes, believe it or not, a couple of my clients didn't know what it meant to surrender) the literal meaning is "to relinquish possession or control." In terms of this process, it means letting go and allowing things to unfold. It's so important to let it all play out, wait for the guy to make the first move, and let him dictate the timing and speed of the relationship. Surrender to the man's process, and also surrender to the Girlfriend 911 process by following the rules. Don't get in the way of it! Don't let your mind get in the way of your heart.

Your mind will screw it up. Get out of your mind, and focus on your heart only. If you do this, you will be able to surrender and reap the benefits.

I had a client who dated a guy that would not commit. She controlled the relationship by getting out her calendar and tying him down to dates and trips, months in advance. She thought that the relationship couldn't possibly end if they had all of these trips planned. It just doesn't work this way. She suffocated him, because it was not organic. Most men are far more free-spirited. They don't like being boxed in and definitely don't like being micromanaged by women. Once this client got on my program and allowed the man to take the lead, she saw great results. She surrendered. When a man wants to be with you, he will contact you. You aren't going to be the one controlling it. If you do, you can kiss it goodbye.

So, *surrender*! Stop trying to control the relationship or him. Remember, you can't make someone love you. He's got to get there on his own. Sit back, relax, and wait and see what happens. Most importantly, this means doing exactly what I tell you to do, step-by-step, and detaching from the outcome. For those of you who don't understand what detaching from the outcome means, it means having no expectation of how this is all going to end up, and having no preconceived ideas. Basically, your future, in terms of your relationship, is a blank canvas. You have no idea what is going to happen, and you're not going to control what happens either. You're going to commit to following my program, and after that, you're going to allow the Girlfriend 911 process to unfold, without rushing it. It'll take as much time as it needs to take to get the desired result, and it's different for everyone. This is a hard one for so many women, as we want what we want when we want it.

You need to completely *surrender* and stop trying to figure out what he's thinking, what he's feeling, what he's doing, and how this is going to work out. It is so much more beneficial to you to put all those thoughts out of your mind, because the truth is that you are not psychic and you don't know what he is doing or thinking, whether he will or won't call, whether he will or won't email, etc. It is so much more exciting to stop all that and wait and see what happens and what he does, without trying to pre-empt it. If you can do that one thing, it will help you to stay in a more stable and happy place. Do not assume you know how this will work out. Do not project scenarios that might not happen. Just surrender and allow the unfolding to take place. The *old* way didn't work, so now you have simply changed the dynamic and you are in your power. Detach from the outcome and *wait and see*!!!!

Another important point I must make is that you absolutely cannot listen to your friends' advice or opinions during this process. Your friends, sorry to say, are most likely as ignorant about this subject as you are at the present time unless they've been through the Girlfriend 911 process. Please listen only to me, not to your girlfriends. When they tell you that ignoring a man's text is rude, or that sending a Goodbye Letter is a bitchy thing to do, etc., I'm afraid they don't know what's best in this situation. Please note that being clear, concise, stating your truth, and telling a man what you want is not being a bitch or being mean. It's being *empowered*, and that is always a good thing.

As I previously stated, one can never figure out the timing on these things. If the guy never responds to your Goodbye Letter and you never hear from him again, that's a *very clear sign* that this was absolutely not the guy for you. As I said, I've yet to see this happen, but you could be the first. If it happens to you, just be thankful that you know the truth of the situation. Now you can start afresh and move on. If he does respond, there is no hard and fast rule about when it will happen. Some respond immediately, and others take days, weeks, or months. Either way, I can pretty much guarantee that they are reading the letter over and over again, all the while processing what you are saying, and trying to figure out their next move.

As I mentioned earlier, when you are sleep-training a baby, rule number one is to let the baby "cry it out" until they realize they have to self-soothe to go to sleep, and you are not coming back in to coddle them. The same is true for men. When you create a standard and a boundary, you have to stick to it and can't under any circumstances give in. Let him "cry it out" so to speak, and do not coddle him. When you write your Goodbye Letter, you are creating a very definite standard and boundary for yourself that has clearly been lacking in this relationship thus far. Now you are saying "here's what I want, here's what I need, and if you can't, or don't want to provide that for me, you can't be in my life." If you stick to that standard and boundary and don't give in, you will force your man to come up to where you are, or you'll get rid of him for good. The only way he will ever take you seriously and do the work he needs to do to come up to your standard, is if you stick to it yourself. Again, if you run back to the crib to pick up your screaming baby, he'll always know he can manipulate you, and will never learn to go to sleep on his own. Training your guy is going to take time, discipline and hard work. He's desperately going to want to go back to the way things were, when you had no respect for yourself, and everything was easy for him. Now that you're the "New You," you absolutely cannot let that happen.

STEP 3

THINK YOU NEED "CLOSURE?" THINK AGAIN

I think it's important to discuss the word that so many people love to bandy about in relationships that are ending—*closure*. It's the thing I hear most often when people are breaking up, "I just want *closure*!!!! I just need to know why!!" No, you don't! No matter what you do, he's never going to tell you and give you the so-called closure you think you need. Men are simple creatures. They are not like us women, emotional beings. They don't like conflict, they don't want to hurt your feelings, and they don't want to sit down and have a long in-depth conversation. Often, they aren't even in touch with their own emotions and feelings to know the true reason why they don't want to be with you. To use a food analogy, they just want to eat their meal, they don't want to know how the chef prepared it, what store he bought the ingredients from, what time he came to work. Did he steam or sauté the vegetables?

Do not look to your man for *closure*. You have to find it within yourself. Write him a Goodbye Letter, state exactly how you feel and what you want from him. That is all the closure you'll need. The New You will be content with the new way of doing things, so it doesn't matter why he wants out of the relationship, why he can't commit, when or if he's coming back. You don't need to revisit anything in your relationship in an attempt to get answers. He doesn't have them, or if he does he doesn't want to talk about them. You'll have closure the very second you take your power back.

Sometimes, the only way to learn lessons is through the mistakes we make. When clients won't listen to me, no matter how much I try to convince them that my way is the right way, I just have to let them do it their way and face the unpleasant consequences.

Zoe was in the aftermath of a three-year relationship and desperately wanted her closure. Even though her now ex-boyfriend had moved out, there were still clothes he needed to pick up and a house key he needed to return. He had behaved very badly, so she sent him a goodbye email explaining that his behavior was unacceptable and ending the relationship. He had responded, expressing some of his thoughts and feelings, but she wanted more; she wanted her pound of flesh.

She insisted to me that they needed to have a face-to-face meeting when he came to get his stuff so that she could sit him down and ask him a bunch of "why" questions. She felt she had to have "closure" so she could move on. I explained to her that everything she had done up until that point— *i.e.*, taking her power back by sending him the Goodbye Letter—was her closure, and he was never going to give her the answers she was looking for.

I also pointed out to her that three weeks had passed since their email exchange, and he had been radio silent. He could've called her to talk, but he didn't. He could've dropped by the house to see her, but he didn't. *Read the signs.* Clearly he did not want to engage at this point. You can't force someone to do something they don't want to do.

Failing to take my advice, she set up a time for him to come over. As a last-ditch effort to try to convince her she was making the wrong choice, I told her if he canceled their meeting, that was her sign: she would know beyond a shadow of a doubt that he wasn't ready for a face-to-face, that it wasn't necessary, and that the timing wasn't right. Sure enough, he canceled. She got the message loud and clear.

STEP 4

NOW WHAT?

At this point in the program you've turned it around. You've taken your power back and sent him packing. You've stopped being needy, desperate, and pathetic, and you've set a high standard for yourself and a strong boundary for him. For a lot of women, this is enough to shift the balance of power and all it takes for them to move on either without their man, or with him if he comes back on their terms. But for the rest of you, this is the part in the program when self-doubt starts to creep in, you get weak and second-guess yourself, and of course you start to think about only the good stuff he ever did and you completely dismiss the bad stuff and the reason why it wasn't working in the first place.

WRITE AN ANGER LIST

To keep yourself on track, I am going to have you make a list of all the things he's done in the past that have hurt you. We do this so that you don't begin feeling sorry for him and end up running back prematurely. Remember, we are breaking old patterns. At this point, you need to dig into your memory bank and write what I call an "Anger List." An Anger List is a wonderful reminder of why he had to go, why you're doing what you're doing, and how he's not allowed to come back until he comes up to your standard.

Here is an example of an Anger List:

1. You called me from Vegas and wanted me to fly out to be with you. I made arrangements to be able to come for the weekend and called you right back to get the information I needed. You never returned my call.

2. You dumped me for another girl you met two days before my birthday. We had reservations to go away for the weekend. You broke the news to me in an email!.

3. On several occasions, I was dressed and ready for dates with you that you canceled only minutes before.

4. You told me to choose items at a silent auction for you to bid on. Whatever you won, we'd do together. That was such a turn-on. We won a horseback-riding day trip and a dinner for two. You never took me on either.

5. We were supposed to have dinner or drinks when I was in town. You ended up at happy hour with colleagues and said you'd call when you could break away. Rather than saying it wasn't going to work, you left me hanging all night without a phone call.

6. You dumped me for a girl you knew for one day. You called me and gushed about how in love you were, as if I was one of your guy friends, not a girl you had been dating for months.

7. You told me that you agreed that we had a soul tie and that what we had was "real." Then you disappeared.

8. You asked me out on a proper date (your own words) and then tried to get out of it *after* I arrived. Your excuse changed from one thing to another. You felt bad and downgraded it to a drink and appetizer in the bar. You promised to make it up to me the next day. You completely flaked on your promise, but contacted me the following week for a booty call.

9. You told me way too many inappropriate stories about your past and the women you have been with.

10. You've let me down and broken my heart repeatedly, and you've never once been accountable for your actions.

We all tend to have "selective memory," which means we block out the bad times and only remember the really great times, even if they are few and far between. Women especially like to look back at the relationship through rose-colored glasses. This is just an idealized version of your relationship. Chances are, for every one amazing night you had together, there were many more disastrous nights. Your Anger List will help you stay in your truth. Remember the reality of what your relationship was, which was *not good enough*.

Now it's your turn to write an Anger List! Take a break and do it now. Make sure to keep it in your purse or close by, so that every time you feel yourself getting off track or feeling sorry for him, it'll be a great reminder why you are doing this in the first place. It'll keep you grounded, stable, and empowered.

GHOSTS OF HABITS PAST

It's so easy to go back to your old ways. I understand that if you've been behaving a certain way for so many years, change doesn't come instantly. It takes practice. You really need to consciously think about what you're doing and how you're behaving and make sure to stop yourself from making the same mistakes—your "Ghosts of Habits Past." At this point, most women begin to find their power and stay in their power, and start to see very clearly the difference between the Old Them and the New Them. They have no problem following the steps as I laid them out, and they begin moving forward with their lives.

However, there are always exceptions to the rule, and I've noticed that a few of my clients have a case of what I call "Feeble Female Syndrome." This is a phrase I use when women actually feel sorry for the guy, rather than feeling sorry about the situation they got themselves into. They forget about how they've allowed this guy to treat them, and about all that they've put up with. I know logically it sounds crazy, but it's true. They worry about the guy's feelings more than their own. At this point, I think it's important to note that this should not in any way include relationships that involve any sort of domestic violence. If you are a victim of domestic abuse please please please seek professional assistance. It's my fervent hope that you'll never need this number, but here is the National Domestic Violence Hotline: 1-800-799-SAFE (7233).

One of my clients, Christine, had a case of Feeble Female Syndrome. She'd been in a relationship for a few years and things had started going downhill. She'd dropped the high standards she started with at the beginning of the relationship, and as a result, her man started behaving like an entitled jerk and walking all over her. When she came to see me, she told me what a jerk he was to her, and how he'd belittle her, and how on many occasions he would talk down to her (remember, this behavior can only happen if you allow it to).

I instructed her to take her power back and kick him out. He'd been spending a lot of time at her house, but luckily still had his own place. She sent him a Goodbye Letter and felt great about finally taking control; however, it didn't last long. She had such a hard time staying in her power. She would say, "You don't understand, I love him and I can't do this. I shouldn't have kicked him out. I think I'm going to call him." I had to remind her to find her anger. I would have to talk her off the ledge daily and remind her why she was doing this, why she had to kick him out, and why he had to be put on the naughty mat.

At some point, Christine let her boundaries back down again, and he trampled all over her. When she became weak, he found her behavior unattractive and started to treat her badly. She allowed it and things went downhill from there.

We have to remind ourselves, it's about *us*, not about them. *You have to change the way you behave to change the way he behaves.* Respect yourself, and he will respect you. Start all over. Go back to square one. Start this program all over again if you have to. Remember, whenever you settle, you betray your True Self. When you betray your True Self, you can never be in a healthy relationship. You can either allow him to continue to behave badly, or take the steps to get your life and your power back.

If you choose the first one, it's because you fell in love with the *idea* of the person you want to be with. But the reality of the situation is the complete opposite. The choice is yours.

Luckily for my client, she is firmly back in the driver's seat. Even though the relationship ended, she is doing great.

CLEAN UP YOUR IMAGE

After you've written your Goodbye Letter, you have to restrict the kind of access your guy can have into your life. Pay attention to how you're representing yourself on social networking sites like Facebook, MySpace, and Twitter. You can't start posting pictures and updates just to make your guy jealous. This means absolutely no pictures of you out partying, or shots of you with your breasts hanging out, or even worse, of you with other men. Don't tweet about the dates you've been on, or how much fun you're having as a single woman. Your man shouldn't have any access to you (or minimal), or know anything about what you're doing. Absence makes the heart grow fonder. If he's following your life hour-by-hour on Twitter, Facebook, etc., where is the incentive to actually reach out and connect with you? If he does have access to your networking sites, make sure all of your postings are G-rated. Trying to play the jealous card simply doesn't work. It may get a rise out of him for a minute, but the truth is that you end up looking cheap and desperate.

One celebrity Tweeted the following, after a very public break-up: "Omg I ran into mystery man at a restaurant last night. What a coincidence! I made out with him again. Now I really *really* want to know his name!"

That's the oldest trick in the book to make a man jealous. It made me sad reading it. This is not how you win your man back. In fact, that's one way to make a guy lose respect for you. The truth of the matter is, when men want out, they want out. It's your responsibility to let them go. If they are meant for you, they'll be back.

FEED YOUR SOUL

Once you've got the man out, whether it's temporary or permanent, you need to feed your soul and stay "busy and happy," as I like to say. This is a time for you to connect internally with your True Self, your soul, your gut, your faith, however you want to put it...and *feed it*. Do things that feel pleasurable to you and don't involve a guy. Pamper yourself, pick up a new hobby, go to the spa, take a vacation, cook, play, have fun with your friends, go dancing, start playing a sport, write, etc... New You should do all the things you enjoyed doing before this man consumed your life in the first place, and you may want to explore new things as well. There's no need to waste any more energy on this man until he is on your doorstep.

Many of my clients ask me if they can start dating again. My answer is always yes, but only if you feel you are ready. And only if that is what you really *feel* like doing. Don't do it just because your aunt's cousin has a guy she wants to set you up with, or your mom tells you it's time, or your girlfriends really want you to get back out there. Dating for the sake of dating before you're ready can leave you feeling lonely and empty. Remember, stay true to *you*. I always caution my clients that if their man is their soul mate, he'll be back. Doesn't mean you can't date other men in the meantime, but don't be surprised or disappointed when other dates or relationships don't work out. It's the universes way of weeding out anyone who's not your soul mate.

STEP FIVE

IF HE REACHES OUT

Our ultimate goal for Girlfriend 911 is to create a New You: a woman who is empowered with appropriate standards and boundaries, who no longer accepts crumbs, who knows her worth and what she deserves. If in this process your man comes back to you, once you've changed your old patterns and behaviors and gotten your house in order, it's imperative that you continue to stay on track.

If anything is less than what you're asking for, or wanting from the relationship, *don't do it*. If he wants to have a drink and talk, you have nothing to talk about unless he can say then and there that he wants the same thing you want. If he can't say this, he isn't ready yet and it's just a manipulation to try to see you. If he's there, on your doorstep, saying he's ready, that's a different story. If not, he really has to go back to the naughty mat. You can't be "just friends" when you want much more. He can't be in your day-to-day life if he's not ready and where you need him to be.

REMEMBER YOUR PERSONAL MANTRA

Your "Personal Mantra" is the speech that you need to keep repeating to your man, reminding him of what you want and the new standards you've now set for yourself. It's important for you to understand that when you say something, *you mean it*, and you have to stick to it. Don't ever cave in, especially during the reaching out phase. Go back to your Goodbye Letter and remind yourself what you want from the relationship. You can also go back to your Anger List to jog your memory. Don't settle for anything less than what you want. Here's an example of a Personal Mantra:

"I want to be in a healthy, monogamous, long-term relationship with you, and if you're not on the same page, you can't be in my life."

This next email exchange is a great example of how saying what you mean and meaning what you say is so important. I can't tell you enough times that your man will only start to take you seriously when you stick to your new standards and boundaries no matter how difficult it is, how much you want to contact him, or how much you want to cave when he reaches out to you and tries to change your mind. If you're waiting for him to commit to a long-term relationship then there's no in-between.

Kate and Mark had been on and off in a casual relationship for seven years. When she came to see me, she was completely miserable and disempowered. She wanted to be in a committed relationship with Mark and he just couldn't do it.

I put her on the Girlfriend 911 program. She sent Mark a Goodbye Letter and he responded that he cared for her a lot, but he wasn't on the same page. He went radio silent for about six months and then he started calling her again. Most of the time she ignored the calls, but occasionally she would pick up the phone and remind Mark of her Personal Mantra. She never backed down, and everything she had said in her Goodbye Letter was still the same all these months later.

Six months after the calls started, Mark sent her this email:

Dear Kate,

I understand that you don't wish to have any kind of communication with me, that much is clear!

What can I say? I miss seeing you so much. I miss the silly conversations and the laughter that we used to have. We did, right? Am I delusional in thinking that you used to enjoy my company? I wish that at the very least we could have a friendship of some kind even a distant one, it would be nice to at least be able to celebrate your birthday with you or to be able to wish you a happy birthday in a telephone conversation. I know the blame lies firmly at my feet and I have not had the opportunity to discuss what happened with you in person, something that you agreed to do at one point, but we never did.

Please give me that chance to explain!!

Mark

It would've been very easy for Kate, after receiving an email like this, to let everything she had learned on the Girlfriend 911 program go out the window. It was definitely tempting for her to write back and say, "I miss you, too, and let's just be friends," knowing exactly where it would lead. For a moment she thought about desperately wanting the instant gratification and not caring about the long-term consequences, but that was how Old Kate behaved, in the past. It clearly hadn't worked.

New Kate knew better, and instead sent this brilliantly empowered response:

Hi Mark,

Firstly, I want to thank you for the birthday wishes, and to let you know I really appreciate the effort you have made with your calls. Although I cannot call you back, I do listen to what you have said.

I feel I need to remind you one more time, this is not a situation I would have ever chosen. I opened up my heart to you last year when I sent you an email explaining very clearly that I wanted to be in a fully committed relationship with you. You were the one who told me that

you weren't on the same page. I guess I am at a loss to understand why you would think you were delusional that I used to enjoy your company. How much clearer could I have been in telling you that I wanted to be with you? You were the one who said you didn't feel the same way!

You said in your email that you wanted to meet to have a chance to explain. I am not sure what needs explaining. Either you want to be with me or you don't. There really isn't anything in between. I don't think there is any blame in this situation—it's just sad for both of us that we are not on the same page. With getting older comes a certain wisdom, and I am finally very clear about what I want. I know I don't want to be your friend, Mark, and I don't want to spend another ten years being the girl you go eat Indian food with and then you go home to the girlfriend. Not anymore! We both know better than that ... how long will it be before we find ourselves kissing in the movie theater and back in our old cycle?

I did agree to talk back in October because I thought there was actually something to talk about, but from a message you left me back then it was totally clear that nothing had changed for you. I think about these months without you, and I know I have made the best decision for me. As I said, at this point in my life you are either in my life in a fully committed way, or not at all. Please don't think for a minute this has been easy for me. I miss you terribly. You are one of the best friends and lovers I have ever had, and it is like my arm is missing. But I am sure you understand that I want to find someone who really wants to be with me for those silly conversations and the laughter.

I wish only good things for you, Mark.

Love,
Kate

Mark didn't respond after that, but Kate was perfectly fine. She had once again stuck to her new standards and boundaries. She had stated her truth and she was totally in her power.

A year later, Mark called her up out of the blue and said I am ready, I want to be in a committed relationship with you. The rest is history.

DON'T GO ROGUE

By this time a New You has clearly emerged. The difference between Old You and New You should be remarkable. Other people will see a big shift in your confidence and vitality. That's because New You is now an empowered woman, in her truth, happy being who she is. Once you've Exited Gracefully, you need to ask yourself what the Old You would do, and do the complete opposite. That's right. Your old ways didn't work, remember? This new person doing everything the Girlfriend 911 way is the New You.

Unfortunately, however, I've learned from experience and the many clients that I've worked with that not all women are made equal. A lot of women find themselves empowered one day, and weak the next. Of course you will probably miss your man terribly. This process is a major game changer. The game changing has to begin with a breakup and getting him out of your life, getting rid of the old toxic energy that was your relationship or situation, and starting fresh with a new set of rules.

A lot of women have a very hard time staying strong and disciplined and sticking to their standards. And almost always, when enough time goes by that they haven't heard from their guy, they want to reach out and go back to old habits and old ways of doing things. This is the part of the program that I call "Going Rogue."

Again, just as Super Nanny uses the naughty mat as an effective way to help discipline and train children to be well-behaved, I like to use the same technique as a way to shift and change behavior patterns in our men. If you mess up this part of the process, it is the same as putting a child in a time-out for five minutes but then allowing them to come out after only one minute. Lacking discipline renders you completely ineffective. Children won't take you seriously if you go back on your consequence, just as a man will not take you seriously when you say he can't come back into your life unless it's in a committed relationship and then you go back on your word.

The good news is that most women who Go Rogue don't Go Rogue for long. They see that when they go back to old patterns they get the same old results. In other words, not the results they were hoping for. They instantly feel miserable and disempowered and get back on the program very quickly.

Going Rogue means misbehaving, not sticking to your boundaries, and falling back on the promise you made to yourself and to him. You said unless he's willing to be in a relationship with you, you do not want him in your life. For the women I've worked with who insisted on self-destructing and Going Rogue, it has *never, ever, ever* had a good outcome.

A good analogy is when you're dieting: You're feeling good, feeling in control and empowered, then you eat one piece of chocolate cake and it's all downhill from there. If you Go Rogue, and your man *does not* give you what you want, you will end up feeling worse about yourself. It's not worth it! At least the cake is temporary and is much easier to overcome.

Under the Girlfriend 911 program, your words and actions have to be congruent. You have to say what you mean, and mean what you say. If at any point you give in and show him your actions are different than your words, he will never take you seriously. He will know that he can always manipulate you and make you change your mind, and then he will never come up to your standard.

Even if you have a moment of weakness, you have to get right back on the horse! When you get used to behaving badly, it's hard to change that behavior, but it's possible. It's up to *you* to make that choice. It's easy to fall back on Ghosts of Habits Past. So keep them in check. Be conscious and aware of them. Make a list of them if you have to. Do *not* repeat old patterns! This is about creating a whole New You.

PEP TALKS

The thing I noticed that helped my clients stay on track and move forward were my weekly, sometimes daily, "Pep Talks." Pep Talks are a great tool to remind yourself why you are doing this, as we often forget. So many women who exit relationships that aren't working tend to fixate on the few great things they remember about their relationship, and instantly forget all the bad stuff. Here are some tools to help you through:

- Pull out your Standards List and remind yourself what you deserve.

- Pull out your Anger List and remind yourself of all the bad things he's done to you, and how he made you feel, and why he can't be in your life until you're both on the same page.

- Remind yourself that desperation, neediness, begging, pleading, and being pathetic are sooo unattractive and such turn-offs. Dignity, grace, and self-respect are very attractive.

- Remind yourself that sending the Goodbye Letter is what helped you get your power back and put you in the driver's seat. It's so important that you've done this, and that you've leveled the playing field.

- Remind yourself that up until that point your man held all the power, creating an enormous imbalance. As a result, you've gotten nothing out of this situation except heartbreak, frustration, shame, no self-respect, and low self-worth.

- Have no fear. This is about you getting what you want, and by doing what you've already done with my program, you will.

- Remember that you've put your feelings out there one hundred percent, and he told you he wasn't on the same page. So now it's up to him to either get out of your life for good, or get on the same page as you.

- In order for him to come up to your standards, it has to come from him. You've done all you can do at this point by laying all your feelings on the line. If he's to change his mind, he has to come to this conclusion on his own, without any interference from you. He needs to feel absolutely zero pressure coming from you.

- You can't make someone love you, and why would you want to? Why would you want to be with someone who doesn't want to be with you?

If all else fails, take a deep breath and say my version of the Serenity Prayer. This is the prayer that is used in many 12-step programs. It supplies strength and calm for those moving through addiction hell.

> *Grant me the serenity:*
> *To accept the things I cannot change;*
> *The courage to change the things I can;*
> *And the wisdom to know the difference;*
> *Living one day at a time;*
> *Enjoying one moment at a time;*
> *Accepting hardships as the pathway to peace;*
> *Trusting all things will be made right if*

I just <u>surrender</u>.

WAIT FOR HIS MOVE

More often than not, you *will* get a response. It's imperative that you wait it out and do all the things I mentioned in this chapter during that time.

Think of it as a chess game. It's his move, then your move, then his move, then your move. You can't make your move until you know what his move is. If you jump the gun and respond first, you've ruined it. He always needs to make the first move, then you follow his lead. That's how you can read the signs and signals he's sending you. Reaching out to you, no matter what he actually says, is a clear indication he doesn't want to be out of your life and he isn't okay with what you said in your Goodbye Letter. If he were okay, you never would have heard from him again. By trying to control the situation and reaching out first, you impede his process. So don't do it. He will most likely respond if you just wait it out.

Getting back to my example of Melissa and Jake. If you'll remember, Melissa sent Jake a Goodbye Letter where she told him in no uncertain terms how she felt and what she wanted. Melissa waited for him to make the next move, and a few days later he responded.

Here's what he had to say:

Melissa,

I have been honest with myself. I have done a lot of thinking, and as much as I enjoy your company and have had a million wonderful times with you the last few years, it is not fair to continue to see you. I do not have the same feelings that you have. You are a sweet and beautiful woman, but we do not have a future together. There are things that cannot be changed, and I am being honest and realistic. I have not met anyone new, I just saw how things were going and had to finally end something that was only going to hurt you worse as time passed. I hate to send this to you as an email, but I am just replying back to your message. I am certain on this and ask that you take me at my word. I wish you all the best and only want you to be happy—I am not the person that is going to do it. There are a million guys out there that would love to be your guy.

Give them a chance, just remember what I taught you and never settle. I am here for you as a friend if you ever need to talk, but I am not the one.

Jake

These letters are so important, because they contain many signs and signals as to where your guy is at, how he feels, and what he's thinking. The one thing that stood out to me so clearly in this letter was that he said "I *am* not the one" not "*you are* not the one." It was very obvious to me that Jake felt he was not good enough for Melissa, not that he didn't love her. Feeling good enough was something that he had to work on himself. She couldn't make him feel worthy. She could tell him what she wanted and then step aside and let him figure out what he was going to do about it.

Jake needed to understand very clearly that she meant everything that she said, and that she was going to do everything in her power to move on without him if he didn't feel the same. No point in doing the "friend" thing, texting and emailing back and forth casually. He had to be out of her life completely and absolutely.

Again, this is the part of the program that I like to compare to child training techniques. When you're training a child to behave, or you are sleep training a baby, the most important thing you can do is **mean what you say, say what you mean, and be consistent.** That's how children are trained, and that's how men can be trained as well.

As I previously stated, the men are rarely on the same page as you, so the response is always something to the effect of "I'm not there, I'm not ready" or "I don't feel the same." That's obvious, or you wouldn't be in this situation in the first place. So prepare yourself for this kind of a response, and don't despair.

I instructed her not to respond, as there was nothing left to say. Jake stated his case, he wasn't willing to come up to her standard, so she let it go and surrendered.

Interestingly enough, after not receiving a response from Melissa, Jake waited three more weeks, and then sent her *another* email:

> **Did you get into your paralegal class? Happy holidays, by the way. I hope things are going well for you.**

I instructed her to ignore this email as well. No point engaging with him if he wasn't ready to come up to her standards. Obviously, if you read between the lines, he might not be ready to commit full-time, but he clearly wasn't ready to get out of her life full-time either.

It's very interesting how men think. Remember, it's Opposite Day. The silence drove Jake nuts, and a week later, he sent the following email:

> **I hope you had a Merry Christmas. Wish you the best and hope you have found a man that will take care of you and your children. I know you will have a happy new year and your 2010 will be great! I don't have your phone number, and this is the last email you will get from me. I do miss you, but I am doing this for your best interest.**

At this point I thought it was appropriate for Melissa to respond, as he was engaging her in a discussion about their relationship, and when a guy wants to talk to you about your relationship, you can always talk to them about that.

Melissa responded by repeating her Personal Mantra:

> **Dear Jake,**
>
> **I am sorry that I didn't respond to your**

email, but I thought I had made myself perfectly clear in my last email how I felt about you, and that I just couldn't do this emotional roller coaster anymore.

Love is not logical, it's not something you THINK about in your head. True love is how you FEEL in your heart. It has no logical reason, just an absolute knowingness about how you truly feel. In my last email to you, I could not have been more honest about my feelings for you. I put all my cards on the table. It took a lot of courage for me to do that, but I did, and I want you to really understand that I meant every word I said. Nothing has changed for me, so in case you didn't get it the first time, let me repeat it:

"There is no doubt in my mind that you are that person for me. No matter what you say, or what you believe, or how you try to push me away, once I met you there was no one else who ever came close or who ever made me feel the way you do."

You can spend the rest of your life trying

to convince YOURSELF that I should be with someone else, that is your choice, but a complete waste of time as far as I am concerned. I don't need convincing, I know what the truth is, and I know what I feel in my heart. I don't really understand why you think you can tell me who I should love and who I should marry. That's my choice not yours. I told you that I love you. I don't give a shit about the fact that you are thirty, and I am not looking for anyone to take care of me.

I am now very clear about what I want, and I am not willing to settle for anything less. I want a healthy, stable, monogamous relationship with someone that I truly love—not in my head, or who looks great on paper—but in my heart, the only place where love really counts. If you don't feel the same way, or are not on the same page as me, there is nothing more to say. I am not interested in having you in my life as a friend—it's just too difficult and painful.

Melissa

Even though he said that was the *last email* she would ever get from him, he continued to email her. Sometimes she responded when she deemed it appropriate, and other times when he would send her useless emails, she would ignore them.

Bottom line, six months later he still isn't ready to commit, but that's okay with Melissa. She is in her power, her self-worth is intact, she sleeps beautifully, she is anxiety-free, and she's gone back to college to start a new career path. She knows beyond a shadow of a doubt that if, or when, he comes back, it'll be in the perfect timing, and they'll both be ready to move forward in a healthy, long-term relationship. None of the toxic head games are being played anymore. In the meantime she's staying busy and happy. She's out there dating up a storm, but so far nothing's panned out.

A couple of weeks ago, Jake requested her as a friend on Facebook, as she had deleted him when she sent the Goodbye Letter. Of course, she didn't accept his request. After all, she doesn't want him to be her Facebook friend. She wants him to be her life partner.

WHEN HE PULLS BACK, YOU PULL BACK

The beauty of Girlfriend 911 is understanding that when someone pulls back, you have to pull back too. You don't ever lunge forward. This is the mistake most women make. If a man starts pulling away, women tend to get kind of crazy and start trying to convince them they are making a *big* mistake. This is the worst thing you can do. Back off and let him do his thing. Let him come to you when he is good and ready. You just need to stay true to your Self. You know what you want, and you made yourself clear. That's all you ever have to say or do. Don't get needy and pathetic and ask stupid questions like, "Why don't you love me?" or "Why are you leaving me?"

I will never tell you to be rude or disrespectful. I will only ever ask you to be straightforward and honest. Don't play the blame game or start name-calling. This isn't about what a horrible man you think he is, it's about how you allowed him to treat you or allowed him to use you without good intentions. Just take yourself out of the situation, Exit Gracefully, and don't settle for crumbs.

Don't ever make a man feel like you are putting him up against a wall or giving him an ultimatum. Ultimatums are saying "you do this or else," but with Girlfriend 911, you aren't saying that at all. In actuality, you're drawing a line in the sand. By creating standards and boundaries, the message you are sending is, "Come up to my standard. I am no longer bringing myself down to yours."

This brings us back to the example of Julia and Dave. This is the couple that is in the process of breaking up over the issue of a "swinging lifestyle." After her Goodbye Letter, Julia waited patiently for Dave's next move. She kept herself "busy and happy," and he eventually responded.

Here's what he said:

Julia,

This really sucks. I've never felt this horrible before, except when I was getting divorced. I guess it's a sign of how much I will miss you and validation that I really did and do love you.

I think what is weird is that you recognize that you as well as me are not in a position to be married for several, or even many years! Yet you expect me to act like the way a "traditional" husband is supposed to......and the fact that I don't want to means you are saying

goodbye.

That doesn't make sense to me. There were a lot of things I loved about being married, and I want to experience those positive things again! There were a lot of things, however, that also made me miserable and bored and stifled. I never want to go back to living a life feeling that way again. I want to have a life that is full of unconditional love and joy and fun and excitement. Excitement in terms of—and especially with—sex also! I believe you can have that and be committed in a loving bonded relationship.

I guess I just want to say that I am not a weirdo like you think. I used to think I was and that something was wrong with me. I am not in some very very small percentage of people alone in my thinking. I am not warped or sick or strange about what I want or the desires I have. I have talked about them in therapy, and they all agree with me....that I am a one hundred percent normal man!

Maybe I am in a small percent of men who actually has the courage to be honest! Like I am with you. Because I love you and would never lie to you or keep my desires hidden or act them out in secrecy in a web of lies and deceit, or addictions like most men (and women)!

There are millions and millions of people and happy couples who are designing a new model for a successful, long-term, bonded relationship. And studies are showing they are happier and less likely to divorce than "traditional" marriages. The word "traditional" refers to what institutionalized religion has imposed on the world in recent history. And I don't believe anymore in any of that garbage or guilt or morality brainwashing or spousal ownership.

This website will help explain what I am talking about. Could you please read it? Not because I want to "convince" you of anything, but maybe so you at least won't think you dated a freak for the last year.

Ultimately, I think I want to find a partner who is open and interested or already believes and finds living this way more fun and exciting. I'm not even sure it would work for me and lead me to a happy marriage relationship, but I at least want to experience and try it.

Honey, I also want to bring something up. If you would like me to return the photo album you gave me, I will. I want you to know that it is the most special and intimate gift I have ever been given in my whole life! I will cherish it forever, whether it's in my possession or not. I looked at them last night with tears streaming down my face. You are so immeasurably beautiful, and I love you so much. And right now I can't imagine us never making love again. It was truly so special always and every time. We did have an amazing connection!

I am really going to miss you tons, Julia :(I hope we can still be friends in the future. I would like that.

I love you forever.

Dave

And here is Julia's final response:

Dave,

I totally agree this sucks and wish it didn't have to be like this, but clearly we are on different pages here.

As I said in my last email, I am looking for a committed, monogamous relationship. I want to be with my soul mate, someone that I am totally connected to emotionally, physically, and spiritually, someone who loves me dearly and only wants to be with me. You are that person for me, but it's hard for me to reconcile that you have the same feelings for me when you want to invite other women into our relationship.

I don't understand what you are talking about when you say that I expect you to "act like a traditional husband." How could I expect that when I don't even know how a "traditional husband" is supposed to act, and we aren't even married.

It seems clear to me from your email that you are carrying around some major marriage baggage. Did it ever occur to you that if you found your marriage to be "miserable, boring and stifling" it was because you were married to the wrong person and that is why your marriage presented itself in that way? Maybe you will think I am naïve, Dave, but I truly believe if you are married to your soul mate, and in a relationship where you grow and mature together, you will never have to experience what, apparently, you felt in your marriage. That is not to say that marriage is easy. We both know it isn't, but if the love, connection and intimacy are truly there, and you are with your soul mate, the problems you will inevitably face are easily overcome.

As for "being a weirdo like I think" again, when did I ever say that to you, or insinuate it? Never. Please don't put that on me, Dave, as it is not true. Obviously, I think you are amazing and fantastic or I wouldn't want to still be with you. If you have desires to be in a relationship with one woman, but then sleep around with other women, that is totally your prerogative. I am not judging you at all, but that is not a lifestyle that works for me. Please understand again that I really appreciate you being so honest with me in your wants and desires. I am trying to support you here by saying that if this is what you really want, you should be true to that and go and find it. But I also have to be honest with you and true to myself and express to you again that this is not a lifestyle I am interested in pursuing. I guess if I were a robot I could understand the excitement of sleeping with different partners within a relationship, but I am not. I am human and have feelings.

The thought of you sleeping with others while we are together makes me sick to my stomach, and I can already mentally imagine the gamut of emotions I would feel—devastation, jealousy, envy, betrayal, paranoia, lack of trust, just to name a few. You can quote me as many statistics as you want, or encourage me to go to websites to check the lifestyle out, but I am not changing my mind here. I truly believe if you are in a marriage and looking for outside partners, then something in that marriage clearly isn't working. And if something in a marriage isn't working, then either you weren't meant to be together in the first place, or you need to take a hard look at what it is and fix it. I don't think seeking outside sexual partners is good marriage therapy.

If you are not happy in our relationship at the moment because you don't find it fun or exciting enough, surely we should be talking about how we could change that and spice things up a bit, but just between you and me. If you are not happy because you are bored with me, or find me stifling, or feel like you are in a rut, then maybe I am not the one for you. I want to be with someone, Dave, who only wants to be with me, who is madly crazy in love with me, and who can't imagine their life without me. If I am not that person for you, Dave, of course I understand. Obviously, I wish it were different. I hope you find what you are looking for, and whatever that is, I hope it makes you incredibly happy, because at the end of the day, we all deserve happiness.

Love,
Julia

And with that, she exited the relationship for good, with absolute dignity and grace. She knew this lifestyle was not for her. No matter how much she loved Dave, she was not willing to compromise herself. Many women would cave and do it just to make their man happy, and in turn, it would make them feel horrible about themselves. If you know that something is not for you, you have no choice but to leave it if you want to be true to yourself—your True Self. With my help, Julia was able to see very clearly that this definitely wasn't what she wanted. She stayed true to her Self and therefore had the courage and strength to leave.

Dave didn't come back. Her not wanting to be involved in the "swinging lifestyle" was a deal breaker, but in the end it didn't matter, as she knew beyond a shadow of a doubt that she did the right thing. This clearly wasn't the man for her, no matter how much she loved him.

F**K IT PHASE

For those of you who are just a little curious as to what the men are thinking during this time, and what they're going through, here are my thoughts as to their process. As I'm not a man, I can't say with hundred percent certainty, but experience tells me this is somewhat accurate.

The best way to describe the man's point of view is to once again compare it to a child who's being disciplined and put on the naughty mat. Nine times out of ten, they don't go willingly, and once on the mat, they can be crying, kicking, or screaming. At a certain point, a miraculous shift occurs, and the child calms down, is ready to get off the mat, and is ready to apologize to his parents. When men are put on the naughty mat, their kicking and screaming comes in the form of what I like to call the "F**k It Phase."

Yes, the F**k It Phase got its name after I witnessed the way one of my friends' boyfriends dealt with uncomfortable scenarios. Whenever her boyfriend came face-to-face with a situation he couldn't deal with, didn't like, or couldn't talk about, he would say "F**k It," put it in a proverbial little compartment, and stash it away. I looked around and saw that women usually like to discuss, dissect, overthink, and calculate everything about the man. Conversely, guys often don't want to handle it, so they simply say "F**k It," and don't think about it again for a while.

With guys, if it requires too much of a thought process, requires too many words, or requires too many emotions, they tuck it away. They put it in a box and stick it on a shelf. They compartmentalize. The thing about compartments is that they don't stay shut forever. Eventually, they open up. After you send your Goodbye Letter, your man will usually respond quite quickly with his "I'm not on the same page" response. Then he'll go into the F**k It Phase, but just remember that it can't last forever. Everything that is suppressed ultimately bubbles to the surface. Don't be remotely surprised if you get nothing but silence for a long time, and then, suddenly, you hear from him out of the blue. This is exactly how it works. Unless he's not the guy for you, this is what you can expect. Bottom line, when they're in the F**k It Phase, they go *radio silent*. Don't be panicked!

Most men think with their heads when it comes to making relationship decisions—and I'm not just talking about the little head, I mean the big head, too. The point is, they *think* love, and often don't *feel* love. True love doesn't come from your head, it comes from your heart. What I've noticed about men who have been on the receiving end of the Girlfriend 911 program is that by their girlfriend's creating standards and boundaries for themselves, and exiting the relationship, the time apart forces the men to get out of their heads (*i.e.*, False Selves), and into their hearts (*i.e.*, True Selves), which is why those that make the choice to come back are now ready to commit to a long-term, monogamous relationship. It's no longer a thought, it's a feeling.

SPONTANEOUS DECLARATION EXCEPTION

When you're in the "Now What" phase, don't be surprised if your guy reaches out in an attempt to connect with you, and you notice a "changed man" for the *better*— someone who is more mature and more authentic in what he tells you.

One of my clients calls this behavior SDE, which stands for "Spontaneous Declarations Exception." She's an attorney, and the legal definition of SDE "permits courts to admit in court spontaneous declarations uttered simul-taneously with the occurrence of an act. The basis for the admission is the belief that a statement made instinctively at the time of the event, without the opportunity for a formulation of a statement favorable to one's own cause, is likely to be truthful." In other words, an excited utterance that is made without time for fabrication. For Girl-friend 911 purposes, this means that when guys are operating out of their hearts—rather than their heads—they're likely to spontaneously declare their true feelings.

Here's an unusual example of SDE. When my client, Trish, exited from her situation, her man was so tongue-tied and incapable of expressing his feelings that rather than responding in his own words, he sent her a link to a song that basically said that he "wanted to tell her about his life, but his tongue was twisted and more dead than alive, and that he was born a broken man." She was gobsmacked when she received his email and was amazed at the effort he was making to at least attempt to express where he was coming from. He had always been a man of few words, so this was definitely a step in the right direction.

In my own situation, after I had gotten Mr. F. out of my life and had stuck very strictly to my standards and boundaries, he told me things he'd never told me before about his feelings for me. This was such an interesting process for me to observe, as when he was in my life I got nada, zero, zilch. I was now consistently authentic, so if he wanted to reach out and connect with me, he was forced to be authentic as well. Even though he didn't come back in the way I needed, or wanted him to, I felt incredibly validated in what he had revealed in his subsequent Spontaneous Declarations.

SECTION 3
IT'S A WRAP

REMEMBER, YOU HAVE THE POWER!

I make no apologies for the following:

- Repeating myself again and again and again; using exactly the same phrases again and again and again because experience has taught me that by constant repetition, these words take form in changed behavior. I have no idea why this is so, but it is.

- Introducing Jo Frost and her Super Nanny child-rearing techniques into a book about relationships. This may seem like the ultimate male "dis," comparing men to children, but for those of you who have seen Jo's TV show, you know her methods come from a place of deep love and concern for the well-being of the *children*. She works her magic to change them from miserable, unhappy, confused, and lost to calm, confident, playful and very, very happy. She does this by identifying the way the *parents* behave as the root cause of their kids' problems and teaching the *parents* how to change their self-defeating behavior. And so it has been in training myself and my 911 Gal Pals; even as we benefit and flourish, so too do the men we love—yes, even (maybe especially), the ones that get away; when we do what's right for us we automatically do what's right for them.

So now that you have my Girlfriend 911 formula, you'll be able to find and maintain a long-lasting, healthy, and happy relationship. The dictionary definition of the word *relationship* is, "the way in which two people are connected." If one or both of you are disconnected from your True Selves, clearly there can be no relationship. This seems to be what is happening to so many of the relationships out there. If, however, one of you is connected to your True Self, that connection is so powerful that it forces your partner to automatically connect to his True Self, and that's when he changes his behavior.

It's really important that you continue to stay in

your truth and connected to your True Self. Think of HER as your own personal Girlfriend 911, your new BFF; that one person inside of you, your inner voice, that knows what's right for you. As my Mom always says, if it *feels right*, it is *right*!!

If you get stuck, remember that if something is not working in your relationship, or you get any sort of a negative outcome from your guy, then you know you've done something wrong, you've taken a misstep, and you haven't stuck to your standards and boundaries. If you get positive reactions from your guy, and things are moving forward smoothly and easily, then you know you're on the right track and that you're completely in your power.

If you've already told your man that he can't be in your life unless he wants to be with you one hundred percent, and he asks you out for a drink and you accept, you have to pay close attention to the outcome. If it turns out to be a disaster, you know you've given your power back to him. "Out of your life one hundred percent," means "out of your life one hundred percent." You can't see him under any circumstances, unless he's at your door-step ready for a long-term commitment. If it's not the outcome you want, you need to get right back on the program and get back in the driver's seat. On the other hand, if things go swimmingly, you're right on track. Keep up the good work.

For those of you who "get the guy" and end up in long-term relationships, it's very important that you continue to always have high standards for yourself, and healthy boundaries for your partner. If things start to go downhill, you are the first person you need to go back to in order to find out why. Remember, healthy relationships start and end with you. Put yourself back on the program. It's never too late to start over. Make the necessary changes to correct your behavior, and he'll automatically correct his. If he doesn't, he has to go!

When it comes to your men, read the signs and take note of the red flags. Do not ignore them. Pay attention to what he says (his words), and what he does (his actions), and let that be the road map that guides you. In the beginning of a relationship, or in the dating phase, always let him take the lead, and you follow until you know the relationship is on solid ground and it's clear that he's in it for the long haul.

To all of you who have taken the time to read *Girlfriend 911* and follow my program, I thank you from the bottom of my heart and wish for each and every one of you a healthy, happy, and balanced relationship.

THE END

───

SECTION 4
TOOL KIT

CHEAT SHEET

CHANGE YOUR BEHAVIOR AND YOU'LL CHANGE HIS

1. Create a high standard for yourself .

2. Create a boundary for yourself and for him.

3. Allow him to take the lead every step of the way. It's a chess game. He makes his move, then you make yours.

4. Don't contact him unless he contacts you first. Don't play games or lead him on if you're not interested. Always be honest and up-front with your intentions.

5. Pay close attention to signs and red flags. Don't ignore them. When you see one, act accordingly.

6. If you're looking for a long-term, monogamous relationship, postpone sleeping with him. Wait until a good amount of time has gone by, and both of you are on the same page, neither of you is sleeping

with other people, and you both want to be in a committed relationship. If there's any doubt on his part, don't sleep with him. If he tells you he doesn't want to be in a relationship, take him at his word and move on.

GIRLFRIEND GLOSSARY

OPPOSITE DAY: When your man says one thing and does another. Men get confused when they feel real emotions and often their words don't match their actions.

STANDARDS: Standards describe what you will and *won't* tolerate in a relationship. Once you create a high set of standards for yourself, you must vow to absolutely never break them. Your list of standards is basically your list of what you deserve. Any time you accept anything less than what is on your new list of standards, you are saying you are not worthy.

BOUNDARIES: Boundaries represent the emotional and physical space you place between yourself and others. It's where you draw the line. Appropriate relationship boundaries put you in a position where you will not be taken advantage of. Remember, we reward good behavior, but there should be consequences to bad behavior.

SIGNS AND RED FLAGS: These are important to pay attention to. They are road maps to guide you and help you figure out what's really going on when your man isn't communicating. Learn how to read between the lines and pay attention to his actions, not just his words.

GUY TIME: This is what I like to call the period of time men take to process and figure things out. The problem with Guy Time is that it almost always takes a much longer time than any of us women want to wait, but with Guy Time it will take *as long as it takes*. Respect that time, and surrender to this process.

LOOTY YOUR BOOTY: A term used to remind you to guard your "treasure." Don't sleep with a man too soon!! In other words, don't let him *Looty Your Booty*! Before you have sex for the first time with the man you're dating, make sure that he's not dating anyone else, that he's taken himself off of Internet dating sites, that he's not sleeping with other women, and that he sees you both moving forward towards a long-term, committed relationship.

SURRENDER: A state of being, in which you relinquish all control, let go of all expectations and projections, and let the process unfold step-by-step. *Don't get in the way!*

EXIT GRACEFULLY: Exiting from your relationship with grace, dignity, and refinement. It's a necessary step in this program. Remember, if he is pulling away, you need to *pull away as well.* If he wants to come back, he has to do it on *his own terms,* because he wants to, not because you forced him or guilted him into being with you.

ANGER LIST: A list of everything your man has ever done to hurt you, so that you can refer back to it often. This is a great tool to keep you in your truth and remind you of the kind of behavior you no longer tolerate.

GHOSTS OF HABITS PAST: The urge to revert back to the Old You may arise. Be conscious of your actions and stop yourself from repeating past mistakes or falling into old behavior patterns and bad habits.

FEEBLE FEMALE SYNDROME: This is when you actually feel sorry for the guy, rather than feeling sorry about the situation you got yourself into. Don't ever worry about the guy's feelings more than own. You come first.

FEED YOUR SOUL: The time and space that I ask you to take for yourself, and *yourself* alone. This is a time for you to get back in touch with your True Self and do the things you used to love doing before this man consumed your life. Or it may be the perfect time to take up new hobbies that you've always wanted to explore.

PERSONAL MANTRA: Your Personal Mantra is a tool used to remind your man what you want out of the relationship. It should be short, sweet, and to the point—a succinct "pitch," devoid of any flowery language or ambiguous pronouncements that could be misunderstood or misconstrued. Imagine you have only two minutes to pitch a client or boss on a particular concept; your future success depends on clearly conveying your idea and nailing that two-minute pitch. It's the same idea with your Personal Mantra. Write it down and refer to it often. You will most likely have to keep repeating this to your man in order for him to understand that you have a new set of standards, and you won't settle for less than you deserve—so memorize it!

<u>DON'T GO ROGUE</u>: A reminder to stay on track. Stick with the program. Don't reinvent the wheel, or think you know better. You can't cherry-pick what rules you do and don't want to follow. It doesn't work that way. Remember, you can't revert back to old patterns and behaviors and expect different results.

<u>OLD YOU versus NEW YOU</u>: New You is an empowered woman, in her truth, connected to her True Self and happy being who she is. New You has high standards for herself and appropriate boundaries for her man. New You is the complete opposite of Old You.

<u>PEP TALK</u>: My good ol' fashioned words of wisdom used to remind you to stay strong and keep your eye on the big picture. If you start to feel weak, and think you're going to cave because you're missing your man, refer back to my Pep Talk portion of the book, and remind yourself why you're doing the Girlfriend 911 Program in the first place.

<u>WHEN HE PULLS BACK, YOU PULL BACK</u>: This is a reminder that when a man

starts pulling away from you, you absolutely have to back off and let him do his thing. Don't ever lunge forward—that's the worst thing you can do. He'll come back when he's good and ready. If he doesn't, that's your answer. He wasn't right for you.

THE F**K IT PHASE: A phase men go through when they are faced with a situation that they can't deal with, or don't want to talk about. Usually, when they are in the F**k It Phase, they compartmentalize the problem and go radio silent. The good news is they almost always resurface. It's just a matter of time.

SPONTANEOUS DECLARATIONS: A legal term that refers to an excited utterance that is made without time for fabrication. For Girlfriend 911 purposes, it means when guys are operating out of their hearts—rather than their heads—they're likely to spontaneously declare their true feelings.

BIO

For years, Jacquee Kahn has been dispensing "Super Nanny"—style tough love to women in need of relationship help. Her no-nonsense, straightforward advice became the foundation for the Girlfriend 911 program. Jacquee began her career at the Creative Artists Agency in Los Angeles, later transitioning to critiquing and editing screenplays. She currently has a number of writing and producing projects in the works. A native of Cape Town, South Africa, Jacquee moved to the U.S. at the age of 16. She earned a degree in English Literature from the University of California, Santa Barbara. She also studied Economics at London University College in England. She currently resides in Los Angeles.

LIKE us on Facebook:	Facebook.com/Girlfriend911
Follow us on Twitter:	Twitter.com/Girlfriend_911
Email Jacquee at:	Girlfriend911@live.com

ACKNOWLEDGMENTS

How do you thank people whose contributions were so enormous that without them there would be no book? I have absolutely no idea and don't feel myself to be up to the challenge at all, but I'll give it my best shot in the full awareness that whatever I say will be inadequate at best or wholly inadequate, at worst:

1. All this would never have been possible without the kindest, sweetest, most warmhearted, beautiful, funny, special, accomplished Lori LePage, AKA "Lori Lori." Not only did you put the idea into my head to write *Girlfriend 911*, but you were there every step of the way. You took pages of my notes and hours of tapes and laid the most unbelievable foundation upon which I could write my book. And then you were my sounding board and idea bouncer and contributor at all times, day and night. The project was only fun because of you; it would have been a very solitary and tedious process without your spark and infectious loving spirit. From the bottom of my heart I thank you for all of this and more.

2. To David Goldman and Keren Engelberg Goldman, my two Girlfriend 911 angels, who stepped in at the perfect time. David, huge thanks for all your help. Keren, my new BFF, thanks for the countless hours spent editing and re-editing. Your contribution has been invaluable.

3. As you will see when you start reading, I frequently refer to "my" program, and it is true that this is a very carefully designed program that I devised after I, myself, had taken the steps laid out in the book and which, to my astonishment, worked unbelievably well. It is equally true that it could never have been proved to be more than a one-time fluke without all of my girlfriends who came for my help and then helped me by testing, testing, testing. I will be forever grateful for your willingness to share your letters, your experiences, and your hearts so that our future sister 911'ers could benefit too from the proof you have provided.

4. Without my own sister, Britt, I would still be sitting and staring at two chapters. I sent out an emergency SOS and she responded. With her usual effortless cool and clever way with words, she rearranged, changed, deleted, refined,

tightened, and in short, made sense out of the meaningless jumble that had completely defeated me. She also found all those little places throughout the book that needed the same firm editorial hand. You hold a special place as My Sister 911. I know you are always there with your loving support, and I am truly unable to express the words of thanks I feel. I hope you can "vibe" them!

5. To my parents, there are just no words to express my sincere love and gratitude for everything you've given me. Mom, you taught me everything I know: from always looking at every situation as positive (no matter how bad it looked from the outside), to giving me the biggest gift of all, connection to my True Self. You taught me how to always live in my truth, listen to my gut, and follow my own path no matter what anyone else said or did. All those lessons became the foundation of my Girlfriend 911 program, and without your incredible wisdom and insight, none of this would have been possible. Dad, you always worked so hard and were the best example I've ever seen of someone who just refused to give up. On more than one occasion you got back on the horse, gave it another shot, and succeeded. That

amazing drive and commitment to always achieving something, no matter how long it took, or how many wrong turns you made, has been incredibly inspiring and helped me navigate my own bumpy journey. I miss you tons. Rest in peace. I don't know two more loving or devoted parents. Without your constant encouragement, love, and support I would never be the person I am today.

6. And finally....This book would never have been conceived without Mr. F., who provided me with the experiences for which I would frequently thank him without in any way understanding why. Now I do.

Made in the USA
Charleston, SC
01 December 2011